Feathers
from
HEAVEN

A Lesson in Awareness

C.C. Ford

Dedication

This book is dedicated to two important people in my life, as well as one very important four-legged person. The first and most important person, and the one without whom this book would never have been written, is my mother. The incomparable words and stories she has sent me through her feathers have been invaluable, becoming a part of my heart and soul. Would I have ever found the courage to put these words on a written page without the miracle of the first feather?

Mother, I cherish the love you have bestowed upon me and I appreciate the tenacity required from beyond the veil to remind me that we can still communicate. Thank you so much for all the feathers!

Randy, you walk through this with me, even when at times you surely must think me crazy. No matter what is happening, especially when nothing I am telling you makes any sense, you still continue to love and comfort me. Most importantly, you always believe in me.

Bullet, my beloved chocolate and tan baby, thanks to you for all the laughter, love, and life you brought to me. There were days when I would have chosen to escape and avoid getting well by staying underneath the bed covers; but you kept insisting that I play, walk, or feed you—anything it took to get me out of bed and onto my feet. You knew somehow that there was a limited amount of time to teach me about finding feathers that would inspire a book. May you and Mother enjoy peacefulness and never-ending happiness on the Other Side.

With all my love,
Connie

Special Thanks

Bobby,
Thank you for your constant support, which continues to encourage me to make the effort to share my life lessons and spiritual experiences with others. I am forever indebted to you, not only for this support but also for your kindness and everlasting friendship.

Connie

Thanks to Katy Koontz, my editor. Bobby told me you were the perfect person to help me and he was right. You filled me with inspiration making me realize I really could do this. Thank you so much for believing in me.

Table of Contents

Introduction

Believing in Miracles

Believing in Miracles

I almost died at birth. The doctors gave my parents no hope for the tiny baby girl they saw lying in the incubator. The Universe, however, had a different plan for their ailing child. It was *no coincidence* that the surgeon waiting for his next case decided to stroll through the hospital nursery to view the newborns. Upon closer examination of the small baby in the incubator, he asked the nurse how to reach the parents. He knew what was wrong with the baby and felt sure his young partner could operate on this child who had been left to die. And that's how this doctor who was just passing time changed the lives of an entire family in the 15-minute span the Universe granted him.

When I was three weeks old, the doctor's partner removed an ovarian cyst from my tiny body. Without benefit of the modern technology available today, he performed a very risky surgery requiring the steadiest of hands. Unbeknownst to anyone at the time, the cyst had kept my pancreas from forming properly.

Pancreatic divisum is a deformity of the pancreatic ducts that causes malfunctioning of the supply of enzymes needed for digesting food and/or production of insulin. It traps the acidic fluid inside the pancreas, causing pancreatitis (inflammation of the pancreas). The pancreas has two ducts, a major and minor papilla. In my case, the major duct is completely closed and the minor one does not work properly because the cyst pushed on these two ducts, forcing them to improperly fold together.

As a result of this birth defect, I experienced acute stomach pain from the time I was very young, although I would not know the cause for decades. Doctors finally discovered my condition during a series of serious bouts of pancreatitis I suffered during my 40s. It was a *miracle* I survived at birth and another miracle I am still surviving today after having had so many acute attacks. Although I live with chronic pancreatitis, I no longer take any pain medication. I've learned to work through the pain when it gets intense by gardening, meditating, relaxing, and basically learning to put my mind somewhere else (which somehow puts the pain somewhere else at the same time).

The ten years between my 40s and my 50s inspired me to write this book. In the beginning, I wanted to write a guide for patients with pancreatic illnesses and people suffering from celiac disease, an inability to digest the proteins in gluten. (I developed celiac as a secondary disease, caused by the requirements of a pancreatic diet.) I initially wanted to share my diet, supplement, and exercise regime.

But as I slowly began to realize how resilient the human body is and that the miracle of healing was coming from within me, I also came to understand that the book I needed to write had more to do with the spiritual connection that exists among the mind, the body, and the soul than about how to manage a specific physical illness.

Today, I am happy to have my physical and dietary limitations because I know without a doubt that this illness is serving a purpose—the fulfillment of which you are reading now. Developing an awareness of things unseen yet seen, heard yet unspoken, has brought me spiritual renewal (and has taken me back to a lifetime of memories and events that I never shared before for fear of ridicule). I now fully embrace that what I was meant to share is the stories of my miraculous metaphysical experiences and the spiritual growth that they inspired, in the hopes that a similar awareness will open up for others. This indeed is my true destiny.

My philosophy for living is all about synchronicity and awareness. There are no *coincidences* in this world. Believe me; *I know that I know that I know!* This book is not about religion. It is about the kind of spirituality that results in a "knowing" that comes with not only recognizing when unusual things happen that we can't explain, but also accepting our awareness of those things as another way of life. After having traveled 50-plus years to get this far, I can say that although my journey continues to be arduous, it is also very exciting. I would not trade it for anything, including perfect health!

That marvelous journey has led me to a series of questions that I now pose to you, the reader. Do we really have guardian angels beside us? Do spirit guides actually exist? Are ghosts real? Do our deceased loved ones leave us messages? Can we communicate with those who have crossed over? Is there a Light in the darkness like no other light we have ever seen before, and if so, can we follow this Light to our destination?

The answer to these questions is what this book is all about.

part one

A Daughter's Awakening

The title of this book was given to me in a meditation on July 1, 2005, and the cover (along with some special touches for the inside) was revealed during another meditation six days later. That afternoon, I made notes in my journal about the cover, trying to recreate in a sketch what I had seen in my meditation and describing in detail what had come into my mind that morning.

I didn't understand the scope of the project at the time, but eventually the book took on a personality and began to develop. And as that happened, I started having doubts about the choice of the title. After all, this book was my baby and the name must be perfect! My doubts grew, and eventually I actively started considering new titles. Why do we go through this human existence doubting what we feel, see, or hear that may be deemed to be outside the norm? What the hell is normal anyway, and who gets to define it?

On July 11, 2006, exactly one year and ten days after receiving the original title in my meditation, I got a sign that I could not ignore. A friend who is incredibly attuned to the Universe called me that morning and left a message on the answering machine. She said she'd had a dream the previous night in which she walked into a room and greeted a woman who was sitting in a chair reading a book. The woman told my friend that she was my mother (who had died almost three years before). Laughing, Mother looked up at my friend and proceeded to cover her face with the book she'd been reading.

"Connie," my friend said on the answering machine, "I don't know if this will mean anything to you, but on the front of the book were the words, *Feathers From Heaven.*" Quickly but timidly she added, "Please don't think I'm crazy! We'll talk soon."

I certainly didn't think my friend was crazy! But the truth was that *no one* except my husband Randy knew I was writing a book, much less what title I had given it. He had never met my friend, and she had never met my mother. *There was no way my friend could possibly have known the book title.* But apparently, my mother did! She continued to be as determined in the afterlife as she was in her human existence.

"All right! I won't change it!" I said aloud to Mother after listening to the phone message. I assured her there was no way I would ever change the title now. I may be strange, and sometimes crazy, but I am never dumb! Mother really does send feathers from heaven, as you will soon read—and she also truly sent *Feathers From Heaven.*

Chapter One:
Ghosts and Spirits

Why do we often ignore unexplainable events? Why do we sometimes get shivers down our spines or feel like somebody is watching us when we know we are alone? Why do people we are meeting for the first time occasionally seem so familiar? Is it *really* the first time or not? I ask myself these and similar questions over and over.

I think life is like a huge jigsaw puzzle, and frankly, I am not very good at puzzles. It always takes me a while to fit the pieces together. Similarly, the answers to our questions about life become apparent only little by little. Even then, we don't always pay attention to how the pattern fits into the whole picture, and sometimes we forget to consider that the answer we are looking for is actually an odd-shaped piece.

Having always had at least some sense of the metaphysical, I am well acquainted with the still, small voice inside and the feeling in the pit of my stomach that gives me guidance. Intuition is a great advisor when I allow it to be (although for years, I tried to push it away or ignore it).

Learning the significance of coincidence came later. Life is truly all about synchronicity—nothing is ever really a coincidence. Instead, our lives are each a beautifully orchestrated pattern of events, just like the music of a melodious symphony. The individual notes may not convey much by themselves, but when they are combined just so, the result is phenomenal.

In this chapter, I share a few stories about synchronicity and how the willingness to change our beliefs can educate us not only about ourselves but also about how those on the Other Side make themselves known to us. These stories span from the time I was ten years old until I reached my mid-40s. Each experience not only unlocked another part of life's mysteries for me, but it also inspired a cascade of new questions! In addition, each event also prepared me for yet another important experience that would happen later on.

It was summertime, and the southern night was so heavy with humidity that it was impossible not to sweat. Like most of her neighbors in the '50s, my grandmother (known to the family as Mamaw) had no air conditioning. Instead, she had a huge fan in one of the kitchen windows that sucked all the hot air out of the house in the evening. It created a cooling draft as the night air was pulled in through all the open windows.

My cousin Casey and I were nine and ten years old, respectively, and on that night, we were sleeping at Mamaw's house. After Mamaw was snoring away in the nearby twin bed, we moved our pillows down to the footboard of our double bed to allow the cool night air to blow on our bodies. The bedroom window was at ground level, so the cool air hitting us directly in the face helped make the night's heat tolerable.

As the night deepened, we took turns lying next to the window. Mamaw was almost deaf and wore her hearing aid only in the daytime, so she couldn't hear us laughing and giggling together. It was heaven for two precocious little girls to be able to spend most of the night awake with no one else to hear. The night was particularly still and the sky was cloudy, making the stars difficult to see. Since Mamaw lived in the country on a farm, streetlights were nonexistent. The only light in the night was the flurry of fireflies.

The farm had been in our family for generations, and the house I grew up in was only about 200 yards from Mamaw's farmhouse. My aunt and uncle lived even closer, in a house less than a hundred yards away. A fence separated their yard from Mamaw's, and a clump of wild lemon trees grew on their side of the fence, filling the night air with the strong scent of lemon. During the day, we children routinely played in the tunnels formed by the prickly but ever-fragrant tree limbs.

On this night, Casey and I were just lying in bed, staring into the night and watching fireflies when suddenly a woman walked out from the clump of thorn-covered lemon trees! Casey saw her first. She punched me and pointed at the woman. Both of us were spellbound. Neither one of us uttered a single word. I don't think we were even breathing! How strange to see someone, especially a woman, wandering the farm at night.

The woman was incredibly petite and wore a long dress with a shawl around her shoulders. Her hair was pulled back at the base of her neck with a ribbon tied in a pretty bow. She proceeded to walk to the fence and open the gate between the two properties. She went through the opening, and turning toward the pasture immediately to her right, she just walked through the next gate. When she traveled through that second gate without opening the latch, we realized she was a ghost.

By this time, we were up out of bed and following along the windows in the house as we watched her. She continued walking in the pasture below. She began to fade as she arrived at the mulberry tree that was standing a few feet from the edge of the creek bank. When she disappeared into the mist of the night, we looked at each other in disbelief.

Casey and I knew better than to tell anyone what we had witnessed. Who would believe us? Besides, how would we explain why we were still awake in the wee hours of the morning without receiving a reprimand? Let's face it. We were two giggly little girls who were supposed to be sleeping. There was no way we were going to wake up Mamaw and tell her what we had witnessed. Believe me, remaining very silent for what was left of the night was simple.

The next day, I couldn't contain my excitement or curiosity! I couldn't explain how or why, but I knew Mamaw must have seen the woman before. That afternoon, I told her what I had seen from the bedroom the previous evening. She promptly burst into raucous laughter, and then she explained very seriously that the "Mulberry Lady" had been walking through the pasture on her way to that mulberry tree as long as Mamaw could remember. I was glad Mamaw didn't think I was telling a lie. I also knew she would keep our secret for the simple reason that she didn't want anyone to know that she had seen the ghost either!

Needless to say, I never tried to climb the mulberry tree again. From the age of 11, I slept at Mamaw's house nightly and saw the lady quite often. I lost something of my childhood when the tree was struck by lightning one summer and was severely damaged. After the tree died and the debris was removed, I didn't see the Mulberry Lady again. Having had that experience at such a young age, I found it rather easy years later to accept other extraordinary experiences without question. Since then, I have always been open to the idea of an alternative existence as well as other metaphysical possibilities.

My second husband, C.W., died from cancer in 1991. About a month after C.W.'s death, I began noticing how our two cocker spaniels, Cookie and Shadow, occasionally wandered around the house with loving expressions on their faces. Looking up toward the ceiling, they would wag their tails vigorously. I knew dogs could see things we couldn't, so I began to pay closer attention to their actions. When they did this, I would look up and comment to the air, "I don't mind that you are here, but whoever you are, please don't upset them." In just a matter of a few seconds, the dogs would revert to normal behavior.

It took me a while to connect the dots that it was my deceased husband who was the one visiting the house. After all, by this time, I had Mamaw, Granddaddy, two uncles, and a stillborn child who had already crossed over. I should have figured out sooner rather than later that of all those people, the dogs knew only C.W. They had absolutely no reason to wag their tails at anyone else.

That wasn't the only mischief C.W. got the dogs into. When C.W. had been alive, Cookie and Shadow loved to sit on the sidewalk and watch him mow the lawn. As C.W. went across the yard, one way and then the other, the dogs' heads would move back and forth in unison, as if they were watching a slow tennis match.

Once he died and I began mowing the lawn, I always left the

dogs inside. Yet several times that first summer, the dogs would suddenly appear out of nowhere whenever I was mowing. I would see them sitting on the front sidewalk, just as they did when C.W. was alive, or suddenly running through the yard to greet me.

The first time it happened, when I approached the house to put them back inside, I saw the rear door to the house standing open. I knew without a doubt that I had shut the door when I came outside to mow. Our dogs were smart, but even I have to admit they weren't smart enough to open the door on their own! If it had just happened once, I would have believed I might have accidentally left the door open. But the door was opening twice a week, whenever I mowed the yard.

Eventually, I got furious and began yelling at C.W. to quit letting them outside! I explained that I was afraid they would run out onto the street. They never came outside again while I was mowing. Did C.W. stop because I had acknowledged his presence? Did he understand the dogs wouldn't sit still for me the way they did for him? Was it the anger in my voice that made him stop? I don't know the answers to those questions. I just know he didn't let them out anymore.

I didn't realize it then, but the Universe was preparing me for my near-death experience about two years later, and even for Mother's sudden spectral appearance, about a decade down the road. After all, if I believed in the events occurring at that time with C.W. and the dogs, how could I possibly deny the truth of my out-of-body experience in the hospital later on—or, many years after that, of the stunning start of my communication with my mother after her death? Although we're not always aware of it, sometimes the Universe works around us to clear the path to promoting future understanding.

The dogs weren't the only way that C.W. chose to make his presence known. He also made use of a replica of an antique oil lamp that he'd given me previously on my birthday. Although the lamp was electric, it looked similar to the kerosene lamp that Mamaw kept for emergencies when I was a little girl. The switch was shaped like a key that you could turn to work the lamp. I loved this gift more than anything he bought me the entire nine years we were married because of the memories it brought back for me.

When I was a child and the electricity would go off, Mamaw would get out her old kerosene lamp so I could see to do homework. Like any child, I was always excited when the power went off because it was an excuse not to finish my schoolwork. Mamaw would tell me not to worry, grab her flashlight, and promptly go dig her lamp out of the storage closet. Darn it! Then I'd have to continue my homework because now there was light in the room again.

Mamaw always reminded me that she had done her schoolwork by lamplight because it was all they had when she was young. She would say, "Be grateful, Connie!" As I grew older, I appreciated the way she made me study and the fact that she allowed no excuses. She gave me that oil lamp years later, and I still have it. No matter where I lived at the time, whenever the power would go out, I would light Mamaw's lamp.

C.W.'s gift was incredibly thoughtful because he knew it evoked the precious memory of Mamaw's oil lantern. With the convenience of electricity, I could now be reminded every day! His lamp performed perfectly for years—until I remarried.

Before his death, C.W., 20 years my senior, made a suggestion about a friend of ours named Randy who he thought I should marry after he was gone—a man who had worked for me as an apprentice optician for a few years. (We had all gotten along quite well together, and C.W. and I had constantly tried to fix Randy up with dates before he eventually moved from Tennessee to Florida to take a sales job with a large optical company.) I got very angry with C.W. at the time for even suggesting such a thing! But, as it turned out, my dying husband's gesture of true love and selflessness ended up bringing the two of us together.

It turned out that Randy missed Tennessee, so he called C.W. to ask for his help finding a sales job back here. C.W. obliged right away, before finally losing his battle with cancer a month later. After C.W.'s death, Randy was a blessing. He helped me a great deal. When I had an accident and was on crutches for three weeks, Randy mowed the grass, took care of the yard, and drove me around on his day off to take care of the business of the estate. He also took me out to eat and to the movies for several weeks, trying to keep me from being depressed. Basically, he forced me into life again. After about six months, we started dating, and after 12 months we were married. And then the lamp C.W. had given me several years before began to do some funky stuff.

When Randy and I would have an argument, the lamp would flicker, even though we hadn't been anywhere near it. Sometimes it flickered on when it had been off, and at other times, it would flicker off if it had been on. When we would stop arguing, the lamp would quit flickering. Many times in the midst of an argument, I would walk away from my new husband to fix my precious lamp by turning the key switch. Sometimes it would respond and sometimes it just wouldn't go off no matter how many times I flipped the key.

I asked my new father-in-law to fix the lamp because he is an expert in electrical matters. I explained about the flickering and told him I thought that the wiring must have a short circuit somewhere. He smiled and explained that a key switch had to be rotated all the way to either the "off" or "on" position to function. It *couldn't* flicker, he told me, because the switch wouldn't allow it to do so. At my request, he took the lamp home with him anyway. When he checked the wiring, he found nothing wrong with it. I made myself a mental note to always leave it off. The very next time Randy and I raised our voices during a discussion, the lamp went on and off. We both stopped and stared at each other in disbelief, yet with a sudden understanding.

Is this really happening? I thought. *Could my deceased husband be telling us not to argue?* Randy and I unplugged the lamp and moved it into the garage. We still have it, but we don't use it anymore. Even so, the memory is a constant reminder to both of us of how C.W. taught us to talk through our differences instead of fighting about them. Through spirit, my deceased husband helped make a new marriage a happy and successful one. Randy and I have now been married for 20 years, so I guess C.W.'s infinite wisdom worked.

After he couldn't use the dogs or the lamp to make contact, C.W. began to use the garage door to get my attention. It began going up and down sporadically. Assuming the mechanics were at fault, I called a repairman. After several service visits, the repairman insisted he had done everything possible to fix the door. He installed a new control on the wall, and I purchased two new garage openers that operated on a different frequency from the original ones. When the problem persisted, I eventually figured out that C.W. was up to his tricks again.

Randy and I could be lying in bed at night watching the news, and the door would begin its familiar up-and-down exercise. We finally reached the point of yelling, "Hi!" to C.W. Then the bouncing door would quiet. The thought occurred to me that C.W. may have started using the door because he hadn't wanted his lamp banished to the garage! Oh well, we don't get everything we want in this life, so maybe we don't always get what we want in the afterlife either. One thing is for sure, though. We always get what we need in order for us to learn, and I was learning to be more and more comfortable about communication from the Other Side.

In all the years C.W. made appearances after his death, he never scared me until one particular evening when I was at home alone taking a shower. Suddenly, I felt a blast of unusually cold air. I always closed the door to the bathroom when I showered so the dogs wouldn't push open the shower door with their paws and jump inside with me. So when I felt the cold air, I looked through the clear glass shower doors to see if the bathroom door had somehow swung open, and that's when I saw the doorknob slowly twisting.

Terrified, I suddenly realized the dogs were not barking. For a moment, I thought Randy had arrived home early, and I hadn't heard him over the sound of the running water. Calling out his name, I got no response. The door started to open, and the draft got colder. I held my breath in fear as I stood watching the door open wide enough for someone to walk through—except no one was there. *And then it just closed again, all on its own!*

The bathroom became so cold that even the hot water running down my body wasn't keeping me warm. I turned off the shower and felt C.W.'s familiar presence. I couldn't see, hear, or smell him, but I *knew* he was there. Not knowing what else to do, and feeling a little silly, I started talking to him out loud. I told him that his daughter was just fine, as were the grandchildren, who were growing like weeds. I told him I knew he would be proud of them. Then I thanked him for watching over all of us, and I let him know that Cookie and Shadow loved his visits.

As I spoke, I stood in the shower still facing the bathroom door. I felt goofy about talking to nothing but air, but I did it anyway! Then I felt the room begin to warm again. Once more, the doorknob began to twist. The door opened and closed again as C.W. went out. By the end of the experience, I was hyperventilating. He'd scared me out of my wits! I turned the hot water back on to warm myself.

It wasn't C.W.'s presence that made me afraid. It was simply the way the entire episode transpired. I hadn't *seen* the door open whenever he let the dogs outside when I was mowing. But this time, I had seen the doorknob actually turn. I saw the door open wide and close again. I felt his presence and experienced the "knowing" of who it was, even though I couldn't see him. I felt the air change from cool to warm as I gave him news about his family. He totally understood me, didn't he? Why was I able to see the turning of the knob and the opening of the door and feel him so strongly, yet not be able to see him?

When I got out of the shower, I called Randy at work and re-layed the story to him, asking him to come home immediately. We tried to figure out why C.W.'s spirit had been so intent about com-municating on this particular evening. Why was it different than any other day? We were at a total loss, because C.W. had done nothing this intriguing or spectacular before. It had always been the lamp flickering, letting the dogs out, or the roving garage door, but never something so personal.

I went to the kitchen to fix dinner. Opening the pantry, I glanced at the calendar hanging inside the door. And then it hit me—today was C.W.'s birthday! I suppose he wanted someone to tell him, "Happy Birthday." So I did. But I also told him he had scared the bejesus out of me and not to do it again! Since then, there have been no more scary visits while showering.

At first when the metaphysical incidents began to happen, I thought C.W. might not have known how to get to the Light. As I began to read about such incidents happening to others, I realized months later that he just liked to visit. He always enjoyed being right about everything, so I guess he was admiring his handiwork as a matchmaker!

I can tell that he still comes for short visits because at times I can smell his cologne. It was a memorable fragrance, and I haven't ever known another man who wore it. Randy and I moved to a new house five years ago, and not surprisingly, C.W. has visited there, too.

As the years go by, I have wondered why I could see the Mulberry Lady but not my deceased husband. Why can I feel his presence and even identify him through a feeling or the scent of his cologne? Why can't I see my mother, but I have seen my neighbor's deceased husband, whom I didn't even know? Is it possible close personal attachments keep us from seeing our loved ones? Is it easier for them to manifest an odor, cause lights to flash, ring the phone, raise a garage door, or just remain invisible than it is for them to manifest in human form? Are some souls more advanced than others and so have the ability to manifest differently?

I don't know the answers to all of these questions, but I truly believe the more open we are, the more our loved ones communicate with us from the Other Side. They want us to know they are still close.

Chapter Two:
My Near-Death Experience

On April 11, 1993, I had a near-death experience. For years, I shared this awesome event with no one other than my husband, my doctor, and my mother. On New Year's Eve 1999, in the last hours before the start of the new millennium, I found myself telling my story at a dinner party that my sister gave for some friends. Long after dessert, the talk began traveling through many interesting subjects, and eventually, life after death crept into the conversation.

After listening to the comments and opinions the others were sharing, Randy encouraged me to share my story with the group. I couldn't believe he was volunteering me to share such personal information. Although everyone there believed in an existence after death, I don't think any of them had actually experienced it. I had no idea that my story would end up verifying their beliefs, nor that sharing the story with strangers would open up an entire new reality for me! Here's the story I told:

Randy and I were dining out the evening of April 10, 1993. I cannot remember what we were celebrating, but we split a bottle of wine, and I ordered shrimp. When we got back home, we had an after-dinner drink—even though I hardly ever have more than one glass of wine or beer at a time.

When I awoke at 2 a.m., I automatically assumed the pain I felt in my stomach was from too much alcohol, although the possibility of food poisoning from the shrimp lingered in the back of my mind. I managed to tolerate the excruciating pain for about two hours before waking Randy. Although I was vomiting, it wasn't bringing the expected relief, and my pain just continued to intensify. I realized something was seriously wrong with me, and I needed Randy to drive me to the hospital.

I sat alone in a treatment room while Randy filled out the required paperwork. I was in a cold sweat and began to feel myself losing consciousness. Afraid I might be going into shock, I stumbled across the room and opened the door to get a nurse's attention. I barely managed to tell her what was happening. My memory of her helping me get undressed, putting me on the examining table, and calling the doctor is a blur. I was vaguely aware later of various doctors who intermittently asked questions about my health history, but I couldn't focus enough to answer them sufficiently. Randy, who I had married only eight months before, didn't know the answers.

Watching my vital signs deteriorate, and with little other information to go on, the doctors decided on exploratory surgery. As I was being wheeled away, Randy told me how much he loved me. Lost in a fog, I nonetheless felt my husband's love for me. I remember the blinding white lights of the operating room as we entered and the chill I felt in my bones from the blast of cold air. Then I recall someone placing a mask over my face as I began to breathe heavily and the bright light of the operating room started to fade.

Suddenly, I felt as if I were suspended in mid-air. Sensing a presence next to me, I glanced over to see two angels on either side of me. They were larger than me and had spectacular white wings with gossamer-looking tips that seemed to emit pale blue light. I don't know if the tips were really blue or if blue light was glowing somehow from their soft fragile feathers.

I instantly felt like a weight had been lifted from my shoulders. My body felt light and unencumbered. The excruciating pain of the last several hours was now gone, leaving only a feeling of pure peace and contentment. Even now, I remember how rapidly those sensations occurred. One second I was in excruciating pain, and the next I was totally pain-free and feeling happier than I ever knew was possible.

I began to watch the group of people below me in the operating room as they desperately tried to save someone's life. While watching with interest, I suddenly realized the person on the operating table was me! I communicated nonverbally with the two angels; our exchange seemed to be an emotional understanding traveling through my senses. I expressed to them my knowledge of being the person on the table as well as simultaneously being in mid-air with them. I knew the angels were aware that I understood my present circumstances.

I *automatically sensed* there was something they thought I must see, and because I felt so secure with them, my natural instinct was to trust their guidance. And following the angels' guidance was so very easy! *They knew that I knew* I was outside my physical body, and *they also knew I knew* it was okay. This sensation was so confusing, yet also so totally comforting!

When the realization of my impending death occurred to whatever consciousness was still available to me, something even more spectacular began to happen! Suddenly, the angels were no longer holding onto me but escorting me through the dark space surrounding us. Even through the vast darkness, I felt no fear. Instead, I found the cool darkness comfortable and serene. I was aware of being suspended in midair within in a tunnel-like atmosphere with a 360-degree view of the universe. I was wearing a white robe made out of a lightweight, translucent material that gently swayed as I moved. It was almost like a body instead of a piece of clothing because nothing restricted my movement. The best way to describe it is to say that it was a kind of gliding light covered by a huge, gossamer veil.

In this vastness I was traveling through, I saw a pinpoint of light in the extreme distance. It mesmerized me and I felt a compelling desire to travel toward it. The closer I got, the more anxious I was to arrive at this amazing light. And then suddenly, I found myself right in front of it! Arriving so quickly after the destination seemed to be so far away was totally incomprehensible to me. It was as if a *zoom!* button inside me had somehow been activated!

Although the light was incredibly bright, I *never* felt a need to shield my eyes, nor did I want to look away. The light had a human outline but no distinct face. It had a very loving presence, and the feeling of love was so strong that tears sprang to my eyes. To gaze in the direction of this marvelous light was an honor, and my heart swelled.

The telepathic voice from this presence was male. It was a deep voice with a resonant tone that was authoritative, yet gentle. A small stream of water flowed between the human-shaped light form and me. Feeling the coolness in the air from the water, I could hear the sound of the stream as the water trickled over the smooth rocks. It was like a melody being played as the water meandered, or was this music just imitating the sounds in nature? I asked the presence for a hand so I could get to the other side of the shallow stream.

"It is not time for you to come," came the reply. "We just want you to know we are here and that you are loved." Feeling as though my heart would break from the rejection, I again begged for the light form's hand in order to cross the stream to the other side. The deep resonating voice replied even louder this time, *"It is not time. You still have work to do."*

In the instant of the reply, the light began to grow dim and revealed a meadow filled with happy people laughing and having fun together, as well as with all kinds of dogs, cats, rabbits, birds, and other creatures. The light gave everything in the meadow a misty, slightly out-of-focus appearance. However, nothing was out of focus about the feeling; it radiated warmth and happiness. I felt like a little girl again, lying in a meadow on a perfect spring day and gazing up at the clouds above.

The emotion began to overwhelm my body, and for those moments, I also felt the wonderful love radiating from all the people I was watching. I had no concept of time, space, physical body, or pain, and I felt only the purest possible serenity. I never wanted to leave this secure feeling, nor did I want to return to life as I had always known it.

As I glance back toward the light, it became larger, hiding most of the meadow view as it grew. Then the glorious, all-encompassing light form stood before me once more. Again, I begged for a hand to help me across the stream, exclaiming that I wanted to come.

"I'm sorry you can't stay because you have more work to do," the form replied. "You are loved. *We want you to know we are here for you.*" I can still hear those words echoing through my heart. And I know what the presence said is true: They *are* here for me. Always.

As I turned to leave, a movie began playing, and I was the star. In mere seconds, various scenes from my life flashed in my mind. Feelings in my heart and body coincided with the scenes I was watching, enabling me to realize the significance of things that had seemed insignificant at the time. The small thoughtful things I did in my life were the ones I saw the most. The behavior I was observing reminded me of something I had always known deep inside my soul: Doing good deeds for others while expecting nothing in return warmed the heart. Intention was everything.

I saw unpleasant scenes, too, but they held no judgment of right or wrong. They held only the emotional pain I had inflicted on someone else—and I could feel that pain, in the same way they did. After the movie was over, the light form reappeared.

"It's time to go," the form said. The angels instantly appeared at my side to escort me back to my human body. As we traveled back through the darkness, I felt a mix of emotions that would take years for me to process.

Why couldn't I cross over? I wondered. *What was so important for me to achieve that required coming back? Am I not good enough to cross to that wonderful place? Why am I spared when other people aren't?* So many questions, so much to contemplate. *Did this actually happen? How could I possibly share this experience with anyone? How could I expect someone else to believe it if I couldn't cope with the reality of it myself? What do I do with this newfound information? How do I walk this path, and where will it lead me?* Questions and more questions tumbled through my brain.

I would spend the next seven years thinking I couldn't cross over to that wonderful place because I wasn't good enough, thanks to my strict religious upbringing. Years before, I had left behind the doors of the church and the restrictive belief systems which served to rob me of my self worth. At least I thought I had. Even after having such a glorious experience and knowing I had more work to do, why did I doubt my worthiness to walk the path the Universe planned for me?

On the trip back from the light, I enjoyed an incredible view of the vast universe. Suddenly, I forgot about all the questions. The stars, the darkness, and the cool air on my face were truly incredible. I no longer wondered where I was going and instead got lost in the joy of flying at warp speed while feeling totally weightless. Talk about the ride of a lifetime! I saw other lights, too, and a netting of some sort that I cannot even begin to explain.

As my journey was ending, the angels arrived on each side of me, seemingly out of nowhere, to escort me safely back to my body. I realized they knew about warp speed, too! I looked at the two of them standing beside me as we observed the flurry of activity that was going on in the *entire* hospital. I felt a sudden jolt, and without even having to glance in their directions, I knew the two of them had disappeared. I just *knew*. Then I was back in my body, in a bed in the intensive care unit.

When I regained human consciousness, I was astounded to learn that six days had gone by. During that period, although I'd been having the out-of-body experience, I had also somehow been aware from time to time of being nursed by my family with words of love, hugs, prayer, and inspiration. I knew they were there encouraging and loving me. Even though I could not respond to them, being able to feel their presence and their love was like a magic elixir.

Sometimes I had recognized the voices speaking to me as I

had recognized my husband's touch when he would wet my dry, crusted lips with a sponge. I can remember being out of my body and looking down over the top of him, wishing I could comfort him and let him know that I was going to be fine. When my mother visited, she would push the hair off my forehead, just as she had always done when I was a child. Once I saw her pull a chair close to the bed, sit down in it, and hold my hand. All the while, I was standing beside her, and we were both looking at me in the hospital bed. How strange is that?

When I was inside my body, I would sometimes hear a voice I didn't recognize but always listened to because it instantly gave me comfort. Somehow I knew the deep rich baritone belonged to someone who was taking care of me. The voice exuded confidence and allowed me to feel healing. By relying on the sound of the voice every day, I began to understand that I was still somehow in a human existence, fighting a battle that without a doubt I *was* going to win.

I did indeed improve. And soon after I left intensive care and graduated to a private room, the surgeon who saved my life walked in and greeted me for the first time while I was conscious. I immediately recognized that it was his blessed voice I had been listening to! I will always feel indebted to him, to his talented genius, and to his soothing voice. I could also feel that the nurses and other healthcare workers surrounding me were not only helping me to survive, but some of them were also truly loving me back to health.

After I was released from the hospital, I told Randy and Mother about the near-death experience. Randy told me he was glad I came back, and Mother shared with me her own story of a near-death experience. In a follow-up visit with my surgeon, I mentioned my experience to him, as well. I had expected him to look at me as if I were crazy or to brush the comment off as nonsense. Instead, he was intrigued. He pulled up a stool and asked me to describe what the experience had been like.

I told him how I watched him working feverishly in the operating room to save me from being poisoned by the secretions of my own body. I described the scene when he explained in depth to Randy what was wrong with me—right down to the picture he drew in explanation. I recounted how he folded the paper in his hand to prepare to draw as he rested the paper on his right knee. A twinkle began to show in the doctor's blue eyes as I continued my story. He knew there was no way I could have known about the picture he drew unless I had somehow really seen it.

I also said I heard him tell Randy, "Her life is now in God's hands, not in mine, and her prognosis is grim." He added that if I lived, it would be because it was God's will and not because of anything he had done in surgery. The doctor's eyes grew wider and brighter as I relayed this detail.

"If only you could have known what I was experiencing while you were saying those words to Randy," I told him. "I was literally in God's hands, outside my physical body, experiencing the miracle of death."

I know this experience changed my beliefs but it also made me conscious that the universe is a huge place. We are only a miniscule spec in time and matter. Yes, there is an eternity. Earth time may indeed be linear, but real time is not measured on a clock; it extends instead to a place beyond most human understanding. Having felt the vastness of this universe and the peace that death holds for us, I am forever touched.

When the desire for peace and tranquility creeps into my life, I close my eyes and relive this wonderful experience. I can do it anytime I wish. Even after all these many years, I can get overwhelmed with emotions when I think about it. *I know what I know!* I know with certainty there is another plane of existence only seconds away. And I know *love is eternal, and it's the key that unlocks the soul.*

Before my near-death experience, I wondered about dying and what heaven was like—and now I have seen it for myself. But heaven through my eyes is different from heaven through someone else's eyes. It's many things to many people. We don't all see things here on Earth identically, so why should heaven appear the same to all of us?

I also now know with certainty that we don't die. The soul is never wasted but continues to be molded into a better spiritual being. I understand we come to Earth to learn spirituality by suffering human endeavors. Our intentions are important, and everything we do and everyone we meet has significance. Spirit (my name for what most people call God) expects us to learn and to do the best we can in this human existence. But there's another existence waiting for us on the Other Side where our souls live and learn forever.

Chapter Three:
Four Angels, Plus One

Angels can appear in familiar guise at the most opportune time. This is merely one more example of the synchronized symphony and the Grand Plan of our lives that I spoke of earlier. How is it that so often we miss recognizing these angels? The first time I met one, I knew she was special, but I didn't fully understand what was going on until our interaction was all over! Even so, the experience left a lasting impression I will always treasure.

On a Friday in mid-May, 2003, I had taken my mother to the doctor. She had felt ill that morning, and her symptoms got worse as the day progressed. Deep inside, I felt that her situation would not end well.

As the doctor prepared to send her directly from his office to the hospital, a serious storm was heading our way. Despite the threatening weather, Mother insisted on going home first to pack a bag. The obedient daughter, I allowed her that luxury, and we raced to beat the approaching storm—one that would turn out to be of epic proportions not seen in our area for years.

The sky was growing dark and cloudy, rapidly bringing an early-evening darkness. I called Randy, who came home from work to drive us to the hospital. The storm was so fierce with blowing rain and wind that I did not trust my eyes to see clearly enough to navigate. Mother was terrified of storms, so I was thankful that once we arrived at the hospital and she was sequestered in the dungeon of the emergency treatment area, she could no longer see or hear any of the fury outside.

Randy and I sat in the main lobby's waiting area. After a while, when no one had come out yet to give us an update, I left to check on Mother's progress. The nurse told me she had been sent for medical tests, so I headed back to the waiting area. As I rounded the corner, I noticed that Randy was standing at the Coke machine, buying a drink and handing it to an old woman. Approaching them, I heard her comment on how mannerly he was to be helping her as she lowered herself into the seat next to Randy that I had occupied only moments earlier. Smiling, I took the seat next to her in a chair that was uncomfortably cool while she remained seated between the two of us.

As the storm continued outside, we were well aware of the blowing limbs and torrential hail and rain that had caused power failures in the surrounding area. I asked the woman why she was out on such a horrendous night. She said she had come because she was afraid of storms, and the emergency room *always* had people in it who she could help. *Does she do this often?* I thought to myself.

I gazed into her eyes, wells of deep blue with a hint of cloudiness. Her wrinkled face was tan, like an old leather hide, and her gray and white hair was wrapped up with a string at the nape of her neck. The woman's tan legs were wrinkled and bare all the way down to her old and well-worn Oxford shoes, scuffed with age, which had holes cut out where the pinky toes were. It looked like she had taken a knife and cut the leather so her toes could have freedom and enjoy comfort.

Her dress was clean and obviously homemade, and it reminded me of the dresses my grandmother wore in the 1950s; Mamaw referred to them as house dresses. A lightweight, scraggly but clean wool sweater was draped around her shoulders. The sweater appeared to be almost as old as she was. I also noticed that the woman smelled like roses.

She smiled at me, and I returned the favor. She complimented me on what she called my sweet smile. After thanking her, I explained that my mother was in a treatment room. She took a sip of the cola and then put the Coke down with one hand as she reached into the pocket of her dress with the other. She pulled out a small snap-shut leather change purse. When she opened it to pay us for the drink, I could see that the purse contained a roll of bills about two inches in diameter and held together with a rubber band. I immediately took the purse from her, snapped it shut, and crammed it back into the pocket of her well-worn cotton dress. Simultaneously, I explained that she shouldn't have all this money with her while traveling alone.

"Don't be worried," she said, laughing. "It's just money. It don't make the world go 'round." Her lilting words still echo in my brain. From her serious expression, I knew she really meant what she said. She knew what was important to her, and it wasn't money.

As we began to talk, I shared my worry about Mother's condition. "I am 92 years old," she said, patting my hand, "and there is no reason to fear death." I replied that I had a near-death experience several years before, so I wasn't afraid of death itself, but I did fear the prospect of my life without Mother in it. I had no idea why, but this woman's presence seemed so comforting, and she immediately warmed my heart and deeply touched my spirit. The entire time we talked, we held each other's hands.

She told me how difficult life had always been for her and

how through it all, God continually provided what she needed. She had outlived her husband, children, and her extended family. She admitted being alone, but she said she was never lonely. The words she said next I have never forgotten:

"Your mother isn't afraid of dying either, because she knows where she is going. *She's ready.*" In my heart, I knew her words were true.

Midnight passed before the hospital staff notified me that Mother was stable and was being admitted to a room. The doctors were still analyzing her test results, however, so we didn't know much more about what was wrong. Randy and I said our goodbyes to the old woman and told her that we had enjoyed talking with her. We left her comfortably sitting in the chair sipping her cola, certain that the other people scattered around the waiting room would watch over her after we left.

As the attendants transported Mother to her room, Randy and I walked slowly behind the gurney. One of its wheels clanged loudly each time it completed a revolution. The chance meeting with the extraordinary woman downstairs replayed in my mind. The wisdom and truth in her words bore down on my heart and soul. In rhythm with every clang of the bed's wheel, I heard the refrain, *She's ready, she's ready.*

Once Mother was situated, she told us to go home so she could rest. Admittedly, it had been a long ten hours, but I was reluctant to leave her. She convinced us by insisting that we needed to check on our new puppy, Bullet. We had left him alone during the storm, and she reminded us that he must be anxiously awaiting our return. It was just like my mother to worry about the dog or about us—or anything other than herself. (As a result of that night,

Bullet was ever after terrified of storms.) Knowing Mother was in the hands of the experts, we agreed. By then, it was the wee hours of Saturday morning, and while the storm was finally over, the city was still in complete darkness from the power outages.

When we got into our car, I suggested to Randy that he drive around to the emergency entrance so we could offer to take the old woman home. But when I got to the waiting area, it was empty. I looked for her in the restroom, but she was not there, either. I asked the two women sitting at the check-in desk if they had seen the old lady leave, but they said they hadn't seen anyone fitting my description. Then I knew! *My gut was talking to me.* The old woman was an angel sent to confirm the feelings I'd had about Mother. I was right, my mother wouldn't be leaving the hospital. *She's ready,* echoed through my mind once again. Mother was going Home, but not back to our earthly one.

I got back into the waiting car and explained to Randy that the old woman was nowhere to be found. I told him I'd figured out that she was an angel sent to prepare me for the fact that Mother would not leave the hospital alive. I shared that my gut feelings about her recovery were not good ones. As we traveled home, avoiding the fallen trees and scattered power lines, the old lady's words continued to replay in my mind: *She's ready, she's ready.*

It took the doctors several days to figure out exactly what was wrong with Mother. As it turned out, she had an enlarged heart and two goiters, but her doctor was unable to operate because she'd also developed a rapid heart rate and could not have survived being anesthetized. We knew she could not live long in this condition, although we had no idea how much time she had left.

It was a waiting game that lasted eleven days.

Mother and I spent what turned out to be her last Sunday together, reminiscing and talking about current world events. She also spoke to me about the importance of keeping our family together after she was gone. As I was preparing to leave her room that evening, I leaned down to give her a kiss and a hug and to tell her that I loved her. I smiled and promised to return the next morning.

"I love you, too," she replied. "But you won't see me tomorrow. I'm going Home tonight."

I instantly understood. Mother was a deeply devout woman who believed with all her heart in an afterlife. Previously, we'd both had near-death experiences and had shared them with each other. So it was not at all surprising to me that she did not fear death and that she would have a feeling about when she would die. This was, after all, what the angel whom Randy and I met in the waiting room had been trying to prepare me for. And now it was almost time.

Mother made me promise to maintain my silence. We hugged, kissed, and cried together, and she spoke about how eager she was to see her own mother again. Even though more than 20 years had gone by since Mamaw's death, Mother missed her and was looking forward to their reunion.

Even though the feeling in the pit of my stomach told me Mother was right about going Home, I found it hard to accept that this would really be the last private moment I would share with her. My mother gone from the life we shared on this Earth? Never! After all, she was being cared for in the hospital and looked relatively healthy.

It just wasn't logical to think she'd really die before morning.

Reluctantly, I left, and as I arrived home late that afternoon, Daddy was in his truck preparing to leave for the hospital. When I asked him where he was going, he replied that for some reason he felt he needed to spend the night at the hospital with Mother—something he hadn't done the whole time she had been there. How had he known to go on that night? Had his spirit guide filled his heart with the intense desire to be beside her at that time? I will always think so. I don't know how those things happen, but I know they do.

Daddy called from the hospital at about 5 a.m. on Monday morning to tell me Mother had had a heart attack during the night and had been admitted to intensive care. I rushed to the hospital to see her. Later that day, when Mother was stable but still unconscious, I went home to refresh myself. All the while, I kept hoping this dreadful feeling inside my gut would go away. While I was in the shower, I began to pray for Mother to experience relief from her pain. Suddenly, a vision unfolded in my mind's eye, as if I was watching a television screen. I saw *four* angels—one at each corner of Mother's bed—and as they picked up the corners of her bed linens, they carried her gently away.

Jumping out of the shower, I glanced at the clock. It was 2 p.m. My sister was supposed to be visiting Mother at about that time. As I was walking toward the phone to call her, it rang. My sister was on the other end, and she began explaining that she didn't get to go in for the visit because Mother had lapsed into what the doctors thought was a coma. I rushed back to the hospital, but Mother never regained consciousness. I knew her spiritual body was gone because I saw her leaving, accompanied by the four angels. Her physical body, however, would remain until the process of human death was complete.

At *four* in the afternoon, I heard the nurses call a code blue for the intensive care unit over the loud speaker. I *knew* it was Mother. I felt it in my gut. My heart aching, I left the waiting area and walked across the hall to the hospital's chapel. I thanked the Universe for the peace I knew Mother was receiving.

In the absence of a living will, Mother was resuscitated and placed on life support. As Monday afternoon turned into the wee hours of Tuesday morning, my father made the heart-wrenching decision to unhook all the life-sustaining systems. He knew she would not want to be kept alive artificially. After the doctor removed all the tubes and wires, Daddy said his goodbyes. My sister sat by Mother's side, gently talking to her as she rubbed Mother's hand while her physical body began the descent into death. I kissed her and told her how much I loved her, even though I knew she wasn't there anymore. She was floating above us, watching everything! The angel sent to me in the emergency room days before had been a warning for me to be prepared, and I was. And the vision of the four angels I had seen in the shower just a few hours earlier assured me that my mother's spiritual body left peacefully.

The visit from the angel in the waiting room two weeks earlier had prepared Randy, too. When I'd called him earlier to tell him of the vision I'd had of the four angels, he understood its importance and met me at the hospital to say his goodbyes, as well. He consoled me as we waited for the inevitable. My mind began to wonder again about the angels I saw in the vision. Did they really carry Mother away? How long would I have to wonder if my vision was real? Would I ever know whether the scene I had envisioned was accurate? Validation came *four* weeks later.

I regularly see an intuitive counselor who explains some of my otherwise unexplainable feelings and experience. He has helped me to learn about my soul's destiny and to understand how the Universe helps us heal our wounds, both physical and emotional. I explained how distraught I was over the loss of Mother and dealing with the aftermath of legal matters and all that went with taking care of the estate. As I began to tell him about my vision of the angels, I shared with him the uncertainty I was feeling about whether they were real or if the vision had just been my imagination.

As he chuckled quietly, his glowing smile began to light up the somewhat dim room, and the twinkle in his eyes touched my heart as I realized that somehow *he knew* the answer to my question. He removed the lid from a ginger jar sitting on the corner of his desk. Reaching inside, he retrieved a piece of notebook paper folded into the size of a business card, which he then placed in front of me.

"Your mother told me I was not to give you this unless you mentioned her death or questioned your vision," he told me. "I tried three times to get the message correct, but she was very adamant it was to be written exactly as she explained." It made no sense to him the way she wanted the message to be written, but she was satisfied with his *fourth* attempt. Reaching down, he retrieved the wastebasket and showed me the three wads of paper inside as evidence.

My hands trembling and my eyes filling with tears, I gently began to unfold the paper he had handed me. I slowly read the message he'd written and began to laugh. It was a message of validation that only my mother and I would have understood.

I now carry this piece of paper in my wallet. It is with me everywhere I go. When people bring up the subject of life after death, I tell them this story and proudly pull out the paper as proof. Written on the paper are these words:

ANGELS ARE WITH
YOU 4-EVER

Out of curiosity, I uncrumpled the three wads of paper the counselor had thrown away, and the message on each one was slightly different. The fact that it took him *four* attempts to get it right was no coincidence—it was the validation I needed. Spirit sent the angel in the emergency room to prepare me for Mothers' impending death and then the vision of the *four* angels who carried her away in answer to my prayer for her comfort. What would I have done without these five angels sent to help me get through this tragedy?

I recalled the Bible verse that says, "Be not forgetful to entertain strangers: for thereby some have entertained angels unawares." Thank goodness I was in awareness and didn't miss this wonderfully orchestrated gift of divine synchronicity. How would I have dealt with Mother's death if I hadn't paid attention to the old lady in the emergency room and been prepared? What if Randy hadn't been kind enough to help her get a Coke and sit down? What if I hadn't taken the old lady's words into my heart? But of course, none of those scenarios were ever really an option. I know because of what my mother told me from the Other Side: *Angels are with you 4-ever*.

Chapter Four:
Hello from the Other Side

Several months after my mother's death, I began to feel her presence in an almost eerie way. Somehow, I just sensed her. I began to notice Bullet sometimes staring into midair while giving a questioning turn of his head. His look was all too familiar. It was the same one he always used on Mother when begging for bites of her Apple Jacks cereal. I felt her rub my cheek sometimes, and every once in a while, the familiar scent of her perfume would linger in the air. Sometimes I'd even think I had heard her voice. But I always pushed myself back to a logical mindset, trying to convince myself it wasn't really her.

I knew communication from the Other Side was possible on some level because C.W. had managed to communicate with me after his death, several years before. When I had shared these experiences of his spirit presence with Mother, she had always looked at me with an expression full of doubt and disbelief. No matter how hard I tried, she had never been convinced of the contact. Although she had firmly believed in life after death, she had refused to believe communication beyond the veil happened. Now I wondered, did Mother know she was able to communicate with me and was she still learning how it all worked? I knew the dog saw her. But would *I* ever be able to?

She let me know in grand fashion two years later, on April 20, 2005. It was early morning, and I had just gotten back from walking Bullet. Randy and I always wear muck boots when we walk the dog, and we keep them in a plastic laundry basket in the garage. So as I returned from the walk, I deposited my wet and muddy boots in the usual spot inside the basket and entered the house. Bullet ran ahead of me to the kitchen, anxiously anticipating his breakfast.

While I was in the hallway on the way into the kitchen, I began to hear bells ringing. The incredible sound was like thousands of chimes ringing in perfect pitch—it was a sound I'd occasionally heard before, although on this day, the bells were louder and there were more of them. I knew these sounds were special and that being allowed to hear them was a gift.

"Thank you, and I hear you," I said aloud to the heavens before turning to the task of opening the can of dog food. Suddenly, in the left side of my peripheral vision, a brilliant flash of light appeared! I wondered what it could be as I began scooping food onto the dog's plate. Logic said it was a reflection from something outside the window. The light flashed again, even brighter this time! I turned to see a brilliant light creating the outline of a human shape, shorter than I was. As I stood staring and analyzing, a lightening bolt appeared within the light's silhouette. It traveled from the head all the way down to the floor.

Overcome with amazement, I dropped the can. Dog food splattered onto the kitchen floor, and the light disappeared as quickly as it came. I reached for a paper towel to begin cleaning up the mess, only to find the roll was empty.

As I made my way to the storage cabinet in the garage to get a new roll of paper towels, multiple thoughts raced through my mind. *I had heard the bells before,* I thought, *but why was the sound so different today? What was the light form? What about the amazing lightening bolt? What had just happened? Did the bells and light show fit together somehow? If so, what did it all mean? Was it a message? If so, how could I figure out what it all meant?* I was fully aware that something extraordinary had just happened to me, and I believed the answers to the questions would come soon enough. But I didn't realize how soon!

When I opened the door leading into the garage, my body froze at the sight in front of the step. *Am I really seeing what I think I am seeing?* I thought. I continued blinking my eyes, as if I could blink away what I saw. My left boot was out of the basket, about two feet away from where I had just left it a few minutes before. And it was no longer covered with mud. The toe of the boot was turned toward and touching the step, as though beginning to step up into the house. Balanced perfectly across the tip of the boot's toe was a brown and white hawk feather, about six inches long.

As I tried to make sense of the scene, I noticed the garage door was still closed! No one could have come into the garage and done this. I was astonished, overwhelmed by the sequence of events that had just happened—the bells, the light form, and the lightning bolt—*and now, here was my boot, and this feather!* What did it all mean? My mind was exploding from all the questions popping around in my head at the same time. Suddenly, I got it.

This is Mother! I realized. *Mother was trying to communicate with me! It was the* left *boot! Mother was left-handed—I get the hint!* As I replayed the entire incident in my brain, I realized that all of it was *real.* This was no coincidence. It was a perfectly orchestrated chain of events.

I began to cry. I stood there for a few seconds and basked in the amazement. I touched myself to be sure I wasn't dreaming! What happened in those few moments was not an accident nor was it a set of random circumstances. It all had a specific purpose, which justified the intensity of the entire incident. It could only be my mother, because the thought of her came immediately into my brain as if it was being planted there. She was verifying her ability to communicate with me. And the fact that it was the *left* boot was the convincing touch, just as she knew it would be.

I suddenly realized that earlier, when I had smelled her perfume, I hadn't been crazy or suffering hallucinations. And those times when I'd thought I'd heard her laughter as well as her voice calling my name—they'd all been real, too. They'd all been her. And on some level, she knew the communication worked both ways. She could hear, see, and feel me, too. Amid tears and laughter, I shout into midair, "I guess you thought all this was funny didn't you?" I loved seeing that Mother's wicked sense of humor had apparently stayed with her, even on the Other Side.

I understood intuitively that this communication process must be opened by an awareness of the senses, as well as an awareness of our heart energy. The heart is a powerful part of the physical human body, but there's more to it than that; the love we feel when we are alive is somehow attached to our soul after death. As spiritual beings, we understand all that is. As humans, we aspire to feel with the heart as we attempt to understand the soul.

After receiving this feather in such a spectacular way, I suddenly remembered that on both of the two days prior, I had found feathers in my yard. Mother had apparently been confident that this would be the way to gain my attention. Both of us loved feeding and watching the birds, so sending the feathers naturally seemed like the perfect symbolic gesture.

More or less to appease myself, I asked her for confirmation. *She answered several days later by placing a matching feather on the trunk of the car inside a closed garage!* To this day, Mother's feathers appear all the time to guide me, gently giving me support and affirmation about various things in my life that I question. And they continue to make me smile.

Our deceased loved ones *do* come around and spend time with us, just as they did when they were in human form. Although Mother had been reluctant to believe the stories I told her about communicating with C.W. after his death, now she was letting me know in a marvelous way that not only did she understand that it had been true, but she also now knew how to do it, too!

Knowing such communication was possible, I always assumed that when she figured out how to do it, she would ring the phone or flicker lights like C.W. did. Little did I realize she'd send heavenly bells and a vision of a light form with a surreal lightening bolt—followed by feathers upon feathers! Now, I proudly accept all the feathers she leaves for me. The collection grows, as do the amazing stories of how they arrive.

part two

The Power of Feathers
to Change a Life

Introduction to Part Two

Part Two is a collection of entries from my personal journals about finding the feathers and how they have come to me. The feathers arrive at times when I need an answer to a specific question, but they also come simply to let me know I am not alone.

Even though I *knew* Mother and the Universe at large were sending the feathers to me, I was at first reluctant to share the stories with anyone. I wanted verification, because I knew people were bound to be skeptical. Why wouldn't they be?

After spending 28 years as an optician, inches away from people's faces while gazing into their eyes, I could then and still can now read a person's eyes like print on the page. As I saw doubt in the eyes of someone when I told them about the feathers, the Universe would send more verification, making me even more certain of what I was experiencing. The element of trust was a difficult learning process. Eventually, as I became fully awakened and completely aware of these gifts, feathers began to drift freely from the heavens, and I readily began accepting that they were intended for me without needing to ask for any verification. As with my near-death experience, I arrived at the certainty that *I know what I know.*

These stories are filled with splendor and excitement that warm my heart. The ability to share them with confidence excites my soul. By welcoming these gifts into my world, I am continually amazed at how more and more feathers arrive for me. Though I no longer need verification, I'm still as excited as ever when it comes!

Before each journal entry, I have included some background information to make the entry more understandable.

The italicized text that follows these brief introductions are actual excerpts taken from my private journals.

1.

Feathers rapidly became a part of my everyday existence. I found them everywhere. Feeling strongly that what was happening needed to be recorded, I began writing the stories down as they happened. I wanted something tangible to read in the future if my memory ever began to fade with age. I wrote the following entry while I was still trying to grasp the reality of receiving the feathers and understand what it all meant.

May 6, 2005

Every time I think life cannot get any better, it always does! Feathers continue to be dropped in my path. I have felt Mother around for two weeks, maybe three. I am confident the feathers, especially on the boot, are from her. I have smelled a scent of iris strongly this week, which makes me know it is her for sure because iris is her favorite flower.

The most unusual feather story of the week happened Thursday morning. Bullet did something he never does—but this morning, it was just exactly what he was supposed to do! It rained hard on Wednesday during the day and into the evening. When we began our walk Thursday morning, he headed in the opposite direction of his normal path. He jumped about eight inches off the front walk and promptly began his morning poop. He NEVER does that because he is aware we go in as soon as he does his business, so he usually prolongs the process. I was astounded!

Then, when I looked at him, I saw an inch-long fluffy feather next to his left leg. I promptly picked up the feather and thanked Mother for it. I was so amazed at its tiny size. I said aloud to Mother, "If this is for me, then let me find another one while on this walk with Bullet so I'll know for certain it was meant for me to find." You know, the Universe must get really tired of proving everything to me!

Next, Bullet proceeded like gangbusters to the side yard, even though it was really wet. He never goes to that particular area of the yard in the mornings because it is so wet with dew. He likes to smell that area in the afternoon instead. He promptly began a smelling process and stopped in a spot with his nose to the ground. I thought he must have smelled a rabbit, but when he looked up at me, there were feathers on each side of his nose—identical in size, color, and fluffiness to the one I already found! I laughed aloud before grabbing them from his nose and placing them in the palm of my hand with the others.

I thanked Mother as Bullet and I went on our way. We rounded the corner at the perennial flowerbed only to find another feather in my path; it perfectly matched the others! I wouldn't have even seen it, but it blew up about six inches off the wet grass as though a draft from somewhere had lifted it up! I reached down and actually caught it in mid-air! There were now **four** small feathers in the palm of my hand! It was as if the Universe was saying, "Do you believe me now?"

Bullet then headed back to the house really fast, as if he'd been on a mission that was now accomplished, and he was ready to eat his breakfast. All of this took maybe seven minutes, although our morning walk is normally NEVER less than thirty minutes.

2.

One day before the second anniversary of my mother's death, I discovered I had lost the feather she had given me a month earlier on the boot. I was devastated. If I chose to tell the story without the feather as proof, how would anyone ever believe me? The feather was such an important part of me now that I couldn't imagine not having it. Not only was my heart aching from the loss, but the feeling of irresponsibility was overwhelming. I was entrusted with something so important and somehow it had escaped my custody!

Prior to losing that feather, I had been keeping all of the feathers in a medium-size carved wooden bowl that had no lid. I assumed the feather must have fallen out of the bowl because it had no cover. *Maybe it floated underneath the bookcase,* I thought at the time, *or behind some of the books on the same shelf as the bowl.* I looked everywhere. I even took the books out of the shelves, looking behind them as I went. I checked under every piece of furniture in the room, but there was no feather to be found!

May 27, 2005

Yesterday I realized I have lost or misplaced the hawk feather Mother left for me on the boot in April. It was such an important gift to me, and I cannot imagine what happened to it. I was in the process of changing my closets for the season when I discovered it was missing.

At the bottom of the cedar chest, I found an engraved cherry container with a lid that my sister-in-law had given us for Christmas several years ago. I put it away at the time to protect the finish. But, the minute I lifted the clothes from on top of it, the growing feather collection called its name. I knew this lovely carved vase would make the perfect home. I promptly asked the Universe to bless it and thanked Spirit for the find.

Not only did it remind me to ask Spirit to bless J [my sister-in-law], but it also reminded me to thank Spirit for the gifts and the meanings the feathers hold!

I promptly went into the other room to put my feather friends in their new home and realized my most precious hawk feather was gone. I searched everywhere that it could have fallen and found it nowhere in sight. I felt sick. No one could possibly understand what this feather meant to me. I was devastated then and still am this morning.

I know in my heart, Spirit and Mother will send another one or show me where this one is. I will probably find it in a place that will have a profound meaning. I asked Mother to help me find it, or if she moved it, to please lead me to its hiding place!

Later on in the day, I found new feathers with the help of Bullet, but none of them were my boot feather. I collected three more during the afternoon walk. I found all of them underneath Bullet's feet! At different times in the walk, he would stop to smell something good traveling through the air. And then when he would resume walking, I would see a feather underneath his paw. (It is all about walking your path, Connie!)

I love the new feathers, but I'm still hunting for my hawk feather! It disappeared one day before the second anniversary of Mother's death! Where could it be? Please show me where it is.

3.

The following journal entries are about my search for the meaning of the feathers. I wondered if anything like this had ever happened to anyone else. I knew it was wise to be careful what you wondered about, because you might just get to find out the answer!

The story of the cardinal is so special because Mother loved cardinals. Somehow Mother had known about the flowers, saw me pick, arrange, and deliver them to her gravesite, and wanted to acknowledge the gift. She knew the cardinals would get my attention because we had always competed to see which one of us could attract the most. She got all the hummingbirds, but the cardinals seemed to prefer my yard to hers. She admired their beauty and their ability to become totally invisible in the colors of my nandina shrubbery. She also admired their lovely red color dotting the snow-covered ground in winter. She loved the way the male cardinal fed the female during their mating ritual. By eating just at sunrise and again just as dusk fell, cardinals filled her favorite times of the day with entertainment and joy.

May 29, 2005

Mother died two years ago yesterday. I was going to take flowers to her grave, but I passed by earlier in the day and saw two funerals were being prepared close by. Instead, I went this morning. I picked spirea from my yard and Brenda's [my sister's] yard. Then I took one of my New Dawn roses and placed it in the middle of the arrangement, along with the iris out of our yard. It was gorgeous and in Mother's favorite colors of pink and lilac. I'm sure she liked it.

Something extraordinary happened when I returned home. As I pulled into my driveway, I saw a male cardinal resting on the limb hang-

ing over the beehive. I noticed his brilliant red color immediately. As I passed, he flew about 30 feet ahead to another tree limb. I slowed the car and continued to get closer to him, and it almost seemed as though he was watching to see if I was following. A cattle fence runs parallel to our driveway, and I drove slowly in fear of hitting him as he hopped from one six-foot section of the fence to the next.

As the wheels of the car touched the concrete and rolled toward the garage, the cardinal flew directly toward the windshield and hopped on the roof of my car! He didn't even move as I pulled into the garage. He even continued to sit there as I got out of the car, closed the car door and walked into the house! I am amazed, but by now, I expect anything to happen!

It is later in the day and I am journaling at Barnes & Noble. I forgot to bring my copy of Ted Andrew's book, Animal Speak. I went to the bookshelves to read about cardinals in the store's copy of the book to see if I could understand the significance of the cardinal incident. The book contains information that has helped me a great deal to understand the animal behavior I have seen since the feathers began to appear. One of the statements caught my attention: "Cardinals brighten the environment....When they appear as a totem, they do so to remind us to become like them. Add color to your life, and remember that everything you do is of importance."

What a message Mother has sent to me! I started to put the copy of Animal Speak back on the shelf with the other three copies when I realized I had been reading the fourth one. (There is that number four again!) I smiled as I began to push a smaller book back out of the way to insert the book I had borrowed. As I removed my hand from the smaller book I was drawn to the title! I knew as soon as I read it that it had been put there for me to find. The name of the book was Sacred Feathers: The Power of One Feather to Change Your Life, by Maril Crabtree. I will buy it and take it home to begin reading tonight.

Same day: 5:25 p.m.

After walking Bullet, I began to feed the birds. On the way to fill the second of six feeders, I found a red cardinal feather. I am so overwhelmed with the feather thing! It never ceases to amaze me. They are such a blessing. I have never found a cardinal feather in our yard. That in itself is a miracle since we feed 24 of them every day. I realize it is verification for me about the incident with the cardinal this morning after my trip to the cemetery!

After finding the cardinal feather, I went to the third feeder to fill it and found a feather that was half black and half white. What am I supposed to be learning from all of this? How do I find out more about the feathers and what they mean? Does the book I found this morning answer my questions? I bet it does or else it wouldn't have been shown to me.

EVERYTHING IS OF IMPORTANCE!

4.

Reading *Sacred Feathers* answered so many of the questions that had been rumbling around inside my head. And the very next day, while journaling at Barnes & Noble, I found *another* book that gave additional confirmation that the feathers were gifts from my mother. The story in this entry happened less than 24 hours after the story from the previous entry, and the fact that it happened on Memorial Day seemed very significant. This story underscores how the Universe always provides the information we most need at the perfect time.

May 30, 2005 (Memorial Day)

I began reading Sacred Feathers *last night. I was so enlightened by this book and so absorbed in the stories that I slept very little. I understand better now about how honored I am to be someone who receives feather gifts. I have a whole new appreciation for their existence and for the connections I've made through them. I remembered reading something in* Animal Speak *while I was here yesterday about how to take care of the feathers. I forgot my copy of* Animal Speak *again today and so I returned to the bookshelf to borrow one of the store's four copies, and I can't believe what just happened!*

Only one day has passed since I was here and handled the four Animal Speak *books. I just this minute reached up to get a copy and found another book about feathers. It was NOT there yesterday! I am flabbergasted yet giggling at the same time. The name of the book is* Feathers Brush My Heart: True Stories of Mothers Connecting with Their Daughters after Death *by Sinclair Browning. I pulled the book from the shelf and just stood there staring at the title in disbelief. Amazing!*

I am back at the writing table, holding this book in my hands and crying my eyes out! I know how much birds always meant to Mother and I know the feathers are her way of guiding and reassuring me every day. I am certain that I was meant to have both of these books. As I sit here reading these stories written by daughters who have received feathers from their mothers, I am so appreciative of the relationship Mother and I had in life and now have after death. Mother, I love you, always.

There's no such thing as coincidence. The Universe knew I needed to see these two books to help me realize that what is happening to me is a real honor.

5.

Several years after Mother's death, we decided to sell our house on the family farm. We would be the first ones in the family since the early 1950s to sell property to someone outside our family. A part of me was reluctant, but the other part was excited and ready to move on and find out where this new beginning would take us.

I had been sick with pancreatitis for several months during 2004. Randy took me to Charleston to see my gastroenterologist at the Medical University of South Carolina (MUSC) the week of Thanksgiving. The doctor inserted stents on that Wednesday. Poor Randy ate take-out food from the hospital for his Thanksgiving feast!

In the early months of 2005, I began a dedicated self-taught meditation practice as a way to escape the constant pain I felt. In the process, my soul began awakening. After Mother surprised me with the feather in April and the other things that were happening began to make some sense to me, I knew everything was moving forward in our lives just as it was supposed to.

Even so, leaving the family homestead was not going to be easy. I had moved back to the house after several years away and had felt enormously comforted by that environment. However, I was beginning to understand that spiritual growth was not always an easy path. I do believe Mother's communicating with me from the other side helped me in this transition. No longer did I see what was happening around me to be accidental. The intentions in my thoughts were being reflected in the world around me. I felt I had a destiny to fulfill, and to help me in that, I was being shown the Universe's extraordinary mystical powers.

Whether or not I fully understood it at that time, I knew what I was experiencing was real, and I could feel a change in my entire demeanor. Trust me, I needed the change. I *knew* difficult choices were coming, and although I was aware that I would need more physical strength to deal with them, I also realized that even more, I was going to need spiritual and emotional strength.

June 9, 2005

After acquiring Sacred Feathers, *I have been receiving more variety. It has helped to read about the colors of the feathers, the different birds they're from, and the symbolism behind them. The book says to always keep the feathers, and it talks about storing them in a dry place. The stories from the daughters who have also received feathers have made me realize how very special these feathers are as they direct and guide me. This week, the feathers are everywhere again. I have found them in the most amazing places. They seem to drop from the sky or even float up at me from the ground.*

I now have five red ones. Those signify bringing health and vitality. God knows I have prayed enough for health and vitality to sustain me right now! I have also found several blue jay feathers that I have never found in the yard before. In fact, come to think of it, I've never seen many feathers in the yard in all the years I've fed the birds.

When Mother began to communicate with me in April, she really meant to be seen and heard. Now that I have this book, I realize the feather I found the other day that was black on one side and white on the other was a symbol of balance. Boy, do I need to be reminded of the fact I need balance in my life! We have begun a serious house hunt. Moving from the family farm will be a difficult decision. I pray Mother will guide me with feathers.

6.

I had been asking Mother and the Universe to return my beloved hawk feather for quite some time. I never doubted for a moment that it would find me again. I just didn't know when, how, or where.

By the time I was writing this entry in my journal, Randy and I had found a house. We also found out from my hematologist that I needed an infusion of iron before my next trip to MUSC for pancreatic treatments on September 13, 2005. I was learning that when the Universe decides to open up a path, I just had to be ready to jog along and try to keep up.

My doctor scheduled me for the infusion, which works somewhat like a chemo treatment, in the early morning of August 19. He did not want me going to Charleston without having a chance to boost my immune system and build red blood cells in advance. I relented, although I dreaded the treatment because it made me feel as though I had a horrible case of the flu for about two weeks. Having had several of these treatments, I knew that any medical or housing decisions needed to be made before the effects of the iron treatment began. I would also soon be facing a recovery time for the pancreatic treatment that could easily last three or four months, and I began to ask myself if I could really accomplish everything I had to do.

Several days before the hematologist called to tell me I'd need the treatment, Randy and I had scheduled an appointment for August 19 with our realtor to sign contracts for putting our house on the market. Following that, we had an appointment at the builder's office to choose materials for the new house so the construction could continue uninterrupted. August 19 was certain to be an eventful day! As I said, I learned to jog along and try to keep up, knowing everything would fall into place.

August 18 was full of anxiety and confusion for me. All kinds of thoughts traveled through my head and heart at the same time. I wasn't looking forward to the iron infusion the following day, nor was I looking forward to the possibility of more stents being inserted into my pancreatic duct the following month. Along with those anxieties, I was also trying to deal with the visions of a new house and all the decorating decisions that needed to be made the following day. Could I hang on and not get lost in the fray?

This journal entry was assurance from Mother and the Universe that I could indeed not only hang on but also accomplish everything I needed to do and come through the stress of it all just fine!

August 18, 2005

I got my brown hawk feather back! The brown feather I got on my boot had disappeared. Every time I told the story after the feather was gone, I never felt comfortable because I physically did not have the feather as proof. Everyone in the family kept telling me that it was not important and that it really didn't matter that the feather was gone. But it mattered to me! I didn't need the physical proof of the feather, but I felt the people I told the story to needed to actually see it.

When I found out I had to go back to Charleston for pancreatic treatment again so soon and I also needed an iron treatment before I could go, I asked Mother to be with me, and I begged her to bring my feath-

er back to me as a sign that everything was going to be okay. This morning, the day before having the iron treatment and signing the contract on the new house, I had been preparing to meditate as usual and went out to the storage cabinet in the garage to get a new candle. **When I opened the storage cabinet door, there on the shelf in front of the box of candles was my feather!** *Only two days ago, I had gotten a candle from the same cabinet and the feather had not been there! Mother put the feather in a place she* knew *I would find it. I thanked Mother, my spirit guides, and all my angels! I had my answers!*

7.

August 19 was as eventful as I thought it would be. Randy and I went to the doctor's office for the four hours required to do the iron infusion. Randy got lunch on the way to the appointment with the realtor. We signed the contracts and proceeded to the builder's office to choose cabinetry, faucets, paint colors, hardwoods, etc. We made lots of decisions that day, even though I was drowsy and not feeling well. I made it through the day still excited by the fact that the day before, Mother had let me know that everything was proceeding according to the will of the Universe! On Saturday morning, the day after all the festivities, she gave me more verification. I was, at that time, always seeking confirmation from her. She always delivered the goods!

August 20, 2005
I found another hawk feather this morning! *It was just like the original one Mother returned to me on Thursday. It was sticking straight up in the ground underneath the bird feeder that Daddy made me years*

ago! Hawks don't use the bird feeder, and I saw no other feathers around to indicate that a hawk had made a kill. The feather looked like it had been jammed down into the ground so it would be found. Instead of just getting back my original feather, I also received another one that looks just like it! I'm sure Mother wanted me to know that all the decisions we made regarding the house were perfect, as would be my upcoming trip to see Dr. Cotton in Charleston!

8.

The following journal entries were made after returning from the trip to Charleston for medical treatment. I thought the remedy would be as simple as inserting another stent, but the doctor told me that I had too much scarring from the previous six stents, so another one wouldn't be an option. He told us the only thing left was very risky surgery, so we came home rather somber and reluctant to make a decision.

In the end, I decided to continue living my life as I had been by maintaining a restricted diet, meditating, and exercising. I vowed to make it through every future case of pancreatitis the best way I could. Realizing the Universe was in charge and the chances of successful surgery could not be guaranteed, I remained content with my current way of life.

September 16, 2005
We got home yesterday from our trip to see Dr. Cotton in Charleston. He informed us he could not insert any more stents, and he sent us to a pancreatic surgeon to discuss two surgical techniques that might be options for me in the future. Neither is without incredible risks, but I am

sure Spirit will guide me about what to do.

We got home in the evening, and I woke up very slowly the next morning. I went outside to feed the birds and collect the feathers they had so graciously left me while I was gone. During the process of filling the feeders, I asked Mother to help me make a decision about my pancreatic treatment and whether I should have the suggested surgery.

I also asked her that if everything including the sale of our house and the purchase of the new house would all work out to leave me a duck feather. I didn't know where she would get one, but it had to be a duck. Having the certainty that all is well and is going to end well is important to me at this time. I am not feeling well and wasting energy worrying is not good for me.

*I went inside, took a shower, and dressed so I could help Randy take back our rental car. When we left the house, Randy went out the door first. As I started to step down, I noticed a **duck feather** lying on the rug in front of the step—in the same place where I found my hawk feather. Straight down at my feet was the affirmation from Mother, received within only 60 minutes of making the request! Her answers always come, some sooner than others!*

*I also experienced a ghost happening while we were in Charleston that I want to record. I really don't think I will **ever** forget it, but I still want to write it down. On the Sunday afternoon we arrived, we drove to Hyman's so Randy could eat. Afterward, we drove to the Battery and got out to walk around and enjoy the winds. Then we rounded the corner to walk the half block to Two Meeting Street Inn, a bed and breakfast that we admire on every trip to Charleston. Someday, we decided, we'd splurge and spend the $500 per night fee to stay there!*

We headed down to the opposite end of the block where we had parked. The next two houses we passed have been under renovation since our first trip in l997. The first was a huge Corinthian-columned Italianate villa. It is in such disrepair that the ornate columns, probably more than 200 years old, are rotting away from their connection to the roof of the porch.

We stood in front of the old house admiring the architecture and trying to imagine what the costs must be for all the repairs currently being made. Scaffolding surrounded the columns, and thick sheets of heavy protective plastic covered the porch floor and windows. We talked about how beautiful the house would be someday soon once the repairs were complete.

Randy began to walk away from me down the sidewalk toward our car. Not realizing at first that he had gone on, I lingered for a few seconds, imagining what it must have been like to live in the house. Once I saw Randy had left, I turned to join him just as I saw a man leaving the house. He was an older gentlemen dressed in clothes like my father had worn in the late 1950s. He wore a thin, very pale green cotton shirt with short sleeves and pin tucking down the front with a pair of light gray, baggy, cuffed pants topping his black and white wing tips. He appeared angry and frustrated.

The man began moving down the path that led from the building to the street, almost at a run, and I realized he was going to enter the stretch of sidewalk beside me at about the same time I would be attempting to cross in front of him. I knew at the speed he was traveling that I couldn't beat him across the walkway in front of his gate. As I looked on, he walked right out of the gate in front of the house. I quickly stopped to let him pass in front of me and stood there for a second while he closed the gate after exiting. I even heard the gate slamming when the gentleman turned to close it.

In the meantime, noticing I wasn't beside him anymore, Randy *turned to tell me it was time to go and saw me come to an abrupt stop for no apparent reason. He looked puzzled. As I began walking once again, I started explaining that I had been waiting for the man leaving the gate to cross in front of me, but Randy looked at me like he didn't know what the hell I was talking about. I began explaining once again that I had been trying to avoid running into the man crossing the sidewalk. Still looking at me like I was crazy, Randy — who had been standing right in the middle of the sidewalk, five feet away — informed me there was no man and that nobody had crossed the sidewalk in front of me.*

I gave Randy a detailed description of the man, but he just looked at me and laughed. He told me I must have seen a ghost. He said he had stood there watching me trying to stop abruptly and wondered what had caused me to break my stride so quickly. "No one was on this sidewalk but you and me," he repeated. "Look around for yourself." When I did, I realized no one was in sight on the block or the sidewalk — nobody was there but the two of us.

I had indeed seen a ghost — at Charleston's Battery in the middle of the day! *The man I saw was very clear to me and solid. I wish I had tried to communicate, but I didn't realize what was happening at the time. Looking back now, I think he was probably very upset that people were working at his house!*

9.

We had put our house on the family farm in the realtor's hands in August, but by mid-October, we had no offers yet. We were beginning to worry about the amount of money necessary to close on the purchase of the new house. Knowing construction wouldn't be finished until March, I felt we had plenty of time for panicking, but Randy was already on the verge!

The feather happening I wrote about in this journal entry was extraordinary because I had given *very* explicit instructions about how I wanted the feathers to arrive in order to be assured they were an answer to my question.

October 15, 2005

*Two weeks ago yesterday, I asked Mother if everything I had been praying about—selling our house and purchasing the new house—was going to work out in terms of the money and the timeframe. If so, I wanted **two** feathers like I had **never** received before and I wanted them to be **given** to me. That was a tall order, but I knew she could do it!*

While filling the bird feeders yesterday morning, I began to wonder about my request. Two weeks had gone by, and I hadn't gotten an answer. I wasn't worried because I knew the answer would come. And by now, finding any feather was exciting. As I picked each and every one of them up, I thank the birds, Mother, and Spirit for providing proof of spiritual existence and communication from both her and the birds.

About 9:45 a.m., my sister called and said, "I put something for you on your front stoop, but I wanted to call and tell you so you would know that I left them and not Mother." I went to the door and there were two feathers like I had never seen before. My huge collection of feathers contained nothing as beautiful as these two. As I always do, I picked them up and rubbed them across my cheek very slowly and gently. Usually when I do that, the kind of bird from which the feather came will appear in my mind's eye. But on this day, nothing happened. I couldn't see any kind of bird!

I immediately called my sister to ask where she got the feathers. Recognizing that they fit the criteria I specified, I also wanted to tell her not to be so sure they weren't from Mother after all. My sister has a good friend who gardens for a living. They share a love of plants and gardening like no two people in the world. My sister had found the two feathers the previous night inside her friend's greenhouse. They were guinea feathers! I had given Mother a tall order to fill and she had achieved it quite successfully, giving me the reassurance I needed at the same time.

When I was growing up, one of our neighbors across the road had guineas, and Mother loved to listen to them when Mrs. Wright gathered eggs. The guineas would cluck, making known the fact that they didn't want their eggs removed. When Mother was a little girl, her Daddy had kept guineas on the farm. She always talked about Papaw having them. He used them instead of watchdogs! Nobody strange could wander through the property without the guineas clucking loudly.

Several years ago, my oldest cousin, who still farms the family homestead, bought some guineas. Mother was delighted! She would go out at the crack of dawn and sit on her front porch in her nightgown, drink her coffee, watch the sunrise over the barn, and listen to the guineas announce the beginning of a new day! So the feathers were from Mother after all, via a friend's greenhouse 40 miles away. My sister and her gardening friend were just the delivery girls!

10.

When I wrote this entry in my journal, Randy and I were still questioning if moving from the family farm was the correct path because circumstances kept arising that made us feel insecure about the decision. Even though we knew in our hearts that moving was the right thing to do for both of us, we still had reservations about leaving the security of our comfort zone. Admittedly, we were beginning to wonder if we could live in a situation with neighbors who weren't family. For the most part, our family shared everything. Did we really want to be out on our own, totally alone without someone next door we *really* knew?

We realized it wasn't too late to change our minds. The contract on the new house had a contingency that gave us an out if our old house did not sell. We didn't want to have to rely on the clause as an escape because we really wanted to move. Several people had looked at our little house, but I had to admit it required the perfect person.

Sometimes life's lessons are hard to learn. We were in the midst of a patience classroom without having the patience or understanding to recognize it! As a result, we were receiving the same impatience we were sending out—the more impatient we felt, the more of it we got back!

During all these months, Mother and the Universe continued to send me feathers for guidance. In this entry, I was starting to learn how important it is to be specific when phrasing a request for guidance because the spirit world can be extremely literal. I was also learning that the Universe can have quite a sense of humor!

Every morning, I would talk to Spirit as Bullet and I walked somewhere on the family farm, with Bullet's ever-vigilant sniffer always glued to the ground for the scent of any animals. There was a creek behind our house where a grey heron liked to explore. The bird spent a great deal of time standing in the water or on the creek bank, but he wasn't always readily visible because he'd often be hidden by the underbrush or even a steep section of the embankment. On this morning, he totally surprised me—in more ways than one!

January 21, 2006

Randy went back to work on Monday after taking a rare weekend off. We discussed many financial matters and potential decorating scenarios for the new house. While he showered and prepared to leave for work, I took Bullet for a walk. On our stroll, I asked Mother to send me a sign that moving into the new place was absolutely *the right thing to do. I wanted to know if the decision regarding the new house was correct and if we would have a contract to sell our current house by the end of January. But I was not specific about a sign because I couldn't figure out how to phrase my request. My exact words were to let the sign just "hit me in the face" so I would definitely know what to do and would know our path was the correct one.*

On Tuesday morning, I walked the dog as usual. We were about three-quarters of the way through our walk in the field when I heard a noise about three or four feet to my left. I turned my head just in time to see the gray heron trying to lift off. We had startled each other, and he was trying to fly away. As he flapped his wings to get momentum, he almost hit me in the face with one of them. Neither Bullet nor I had seen the heron prior to his attempt to get airborne, and the bird's sudden movement so scared Bullet that he ran underneath my legs for protection.

Once back at the house, I related the story to Randy, vividly describing how really big a heron's wingspan looks when you are about four feet away and their wings are fully open. I felt so small, and poor Bullet must have felt as tiny as a field mouse! Randy left for work laughing about Bullet.

After Bullet and I got breakfast, I went into the sunroom. I was sitting sipping coffee when suddenly my vacant stare was brought to attention by a hawk that flew out of nowhere onto the ground beneath one of the bird feeders. He had no bird in his talons. He proceeded to spread out his wings and tail feathers. I had never seen a hawk do this, and I grabbed the binoculars even though he was probably only 20 yards away. He was a red-shouldered hawk, and the feathers were exactly like the two hawk feathers Mother had left me! After he flew away, I went outside to see if he had left a feather but found none.

Later in the day, I looked up heron in Ted Andrews' book, **Animal Speak**. I figured that because I had never encountered a heron so closely before, maybe I was supposed to find guidance in the symbolic meaning of heron. I read that people with heron totems are jacks of all trades, which enables them to follow their own path. At the time, nothing really clicked for me in the information.

Wednesday passed by uneventfully, and I still waited and begged the Universe for a sign to hit me in the face! Finally, on Thursday evening, it nearly did! At twilight, Randy and I took Bullet walking in the field. All of a sudden, we heard a sound behind us. I turned around just in time to drop to my knees to avoid a hawk that was about to fly directly into my forehead! I still don't know how I managed to react so fast. Bullet was terrified, and Randy shouted at me that the dove had almost hit me.

"It wasn't a dove," I responded. "It was a hawk!" I pointed to where the bird had flown to a tree limb about 25 feet away. Upon landing, it looked back in our direction. Randy agreed after a better look that it was a hawk after all. About ten seconds elapsed before he asked me, "Are you all right?" I nodded, and we looked back toward the hawk—but the bird had vanished! He hadn't just flown off—he was nowhere to be seen, either in the sky or on any of the other trees (and since it was winter and the trees were bare, he would have been easily visible).

I began to laugh, but Randy did not welcome my laughter. He looked at me questioningly and said, "He almost flew into your face and *both of you could have been hurt!" THAT is when I finally got it— I had asked Mother for a "hit me in the face" sign, and she had just provided one! I explained to Randy about making the request on Monday. On our way back to the farmhouse, I told him I was sure that a hawk feather would show up before we got home. As we crossed the bridge over the creek and got to our concrete driveway, I saw a small fuzzy brown and white hawk feather lying there. I picked it up and turned toward him. He just said, "Well, I'll be damned!"*

I knew when I touched the feather that I had my answer. But it wasn't until later in the evening while enjoying a bubble bath that I realized Mother had been trying to deliver the message for three days. I had been oblivious! She had first tried to send the message with the heron, without actually hitting me in the face (just getting close), but I had been totally unaware. And the passage in the book talked about following your own path, but I didn't recognize it as guidance.

Then it dawned on me that both the heron and the hawk under the bird feeder had both spread their wings right in front of me—a sign to spread my own wings and leave the family farm! Why hadn't I seen it? Apparently, I had to wait to be almost hit in the forehead by a hawk in mid-flight at twilight before I understood! Mother had done everything she could to send the message without literally hitting me in the face, trying diligently to formulate the message without injury.

When I explained the entire scenario of all the encounters to Randy later in the evening, he was amazed. I guess by now though, he had seen so many incidents that he just accepted them as a fact of life and moved on. He did, however, ask me from now on not to ask for signs that could possibly result in bodily harm.

Thanks, Mother, for the verification that leaving the farm is the right thing to do, whether we sell or rent the old house. With a great deal of gratitude, I thank Spirit for showing me about awareness and for teaching me that I can rely on your help and existence.

We ended up selling the house the very next week and moved into our new location in March 2006. And we have continued to spread our wings since then. We moved *again* in 2010, and we are currently looking into moving *yet again* — and each time, we learn to spread our wings a little farther. Through each move, Mother's presence continues in each house we live in.

Writing this book is yet *another* example of me spreading my wings. I can't imagine that prior to the move from the farm I would ever have shared these stories outside the family. Apparently, I had to *move* outside the family to *share* outside the family. I can't wait to find out where Randy and I end up when we get to our full wingspan!

11.

My journal is missing many entries for 2007. My father was diagnosed with cancer in mid-2006 but remained relatively healthy until July 2007. He crossed over to the Other Side in December of that year. I was very sick with pancreatitis and hospitalized several times during his illness. I concentrated most of my energy on my dad and also on trying to help my sister, whose devotion to my father's care was extraordinary, as much as was possible. Mother was ever-present throughout these months, supplying feathers that would always put a much-needed smile on my face. These feather deliveries serve to remind me that the world would eventually get back to normal and that I could always find something to smile about.

When I wrote this journal entry, I was beginning to get some rest from the previous year, but it was still an upsetting time for all of us. The feathers not only made me laugh, but they also reminded me about living in the moment. I found mourning for my dad was a different kind of feeling than mourning for Mother. It was difficult for me to deal with both parents being gone from this human lifetime, but Mother was ever vigilant about showing me that she was always only seconds away.

February 22, 2008

It is a gloomy overcast day, so typical of East Tennessee in the winter. A fine mist of rain feels like it could turn to deluge at any moment. As I sit by the window gazing at the traffic passing Barnes & Noble, where I am writing, I wonder if any of the drivers on the street are living in the moment. I guess the same question could be asked of the people in the bookstore, too, including me.

I got some feathers from Mother this week for the first time in what seems like months! I know it hasn't really been that long, but since Daddy died I have been busy handling the bills, etc. I have not been writing as much, nor have I been writing about every feather I get.

This Tuesday, Mother sent three white ones that I found under an evergreen shrub that Bullet was peeing beside. I looked down at him and saw one feather not even a half-inch long protruding from the bush's branches hanging on the ground. As I reached to get it, the thought flashed in my mind that there were three feathers. Sure enough, when I picked up the branch I found two more. Thank goodness Bullet had peed on the other side of the branch!

I thanked Mother aloud and asked how she had known Bullet would go to that particular shrub. I know there are no coincidences. He probably saw her and just walked up to the bush and peed where she told him. After all, he does pee on command.

Wednesday was a cold blustery day with snowflakes falling from a cloudy gray sky. The wind-chill was in the teens. Bullet loves walking when the wind is blowing fast. He loves to sniff at the smells the wind brings, and on this day, he managed to lead me on a 45-minute expedition! I complained to him about the cold but his four little furry legs kept on moving.

When we came back into the house, it felt so good and warm to my blistered cheeks and cold nose. I put Bullet's leash in the basket where I keep it with his harness, but left the harness on the floor while I took off all my outer garments and put them away. I couldn't stand the harness being out of place, and somewhere in the house, my Mother's spirit was laughing about my passion for order. When I went to pick up the harness to put it in the basket, too, I found a two-inch long white feather on the floor in front of the basket. It had not been there just seconds earlier. I couldn't have missed seeing it even if I had tried! I laughed aloud and thanked Mother for the joy she gives me by reminding me all the time about the neat-nick quirks that I so richly inherited from her!

Through the spirits visiting my house and Mother's communication through feathers, I am forever reminded about living in the moment. I am reminded of how thin the veil between this world and the spirit world really is. I am reminded of how fortunate I am to have learned that we have the ability to be in touch with our loved ones on the Other Side at any moment in time. **There is a truth in the meaning of the word eternity.**

12.

Daddy died on December 15, 2007, and my pancreatitis continued to plague me into 2008. March 18th was my dad's birth date, and that year would be the first one without him. The year before he had turned 80 and, knowing his cancer was terminal, we had given him a big party. We invited everyone on both sides of the family, special friends, and people he had known for years. Even though he was a quiet man, he loved being the center of attention on this day. He wasn't feeling great, but he took it all in stride and loved all the loot and love. That same date one year later would turn out to be a very different day for me. It started with a sign from Mother.

Mother had always flipped the television channel when she wanted us to know she was around. It was not unusual for us to be watching something on television and suddenly have the channel switch to QVC. Sometimes when company was over, they would get really confused. If they were open-minded friends, we admitted it was Mother. If not, we just acted as surprised as they did!

On the day I was journaling about, Mother was visiting for more reasons than one. She was reminding me of Daddy's birthday, and later she was letting me know that she was watching over me and would see that I'd get safely to the doctor's office when I needed help.

March 24, 2008

This happened to me on March 18, but I'm writing on the 24th because I was in the hospital at the time. March 18 was Daddy's birthday. He died in December and would have been 81 this year.

I woke up that morning feeling just fine and with a full day ahead of me. I had an appointment later in the morning to finally begin physical therapy on my hip and sacroiliac joint. My problem with the sacroiliac joint was never completely corrected because of Daddy's illness. (I just didn't have the time then to worry about the pain in my hips.) After that, I was scheduled to see the gastroenterologist to discuss the possibility that my pancreatitis might be an autoimmune problem.

While having breakfast, I noticed the television channel kept jumping to QVC on its own. The remote control was nowhere near me the first time, so I had to get up from my chair and find it. But the channel kept flipping back over to QVC—this happened four or five times. After a few sips of coffee began to wake me up, I remembered the date. I said "Good morning!" to Mother and "Happy birthday!" to Daddy. Then I sipped a little more coffee to help me wake up enough to walk Bullet. It was already shaping up to be a rather interesting day.

After breakfast, I began to feel just slightly dizzy and somewhat nauseous. While I was walking Bullet, the dizziness progressed rapidly and I began to feel like a pancreatitis attack was coming on, although I didn't have any of the stomach pain that I usually experienced with my familiar symptoms.

I was able to drive to physical therapy just fine, but when I got out of the car, I got incredibly nauseated and even dizzier! When the therapist helped me to lie flat on the bed, the room began to spin! It was spinning like it does when you have had one too many and you have to put one foot solidly on the floor to make the spinning stop. When the vomiting began, I knew I had been right about the pancreatitis attack.

I rested, waiting for the wave of nausea to leave. Then I made my way to the car and called Randy. I asked him to call the gastroenterologist and let him know that I was very sick. I thought about how convenient it was that I already had the appointment with him and was only three miles *away from his office.*

As I was about to drive out of the parking garage at the physical therapy center, another wave of nausea hit me. I quickly put the car in park, jumped out, and found a fire hydrant to hold on to as I emptied my stomach once again on a patch of grass. Staggering back to the car, I turned around to sit in the back seat facing outward with my feet on the grass. I reached onto the floorboard for wet wipes. As I opened my eyes after wiping off my face, there it was—a pure white feather about four inches long right beside my left foot.

Mother was right there on my left side, as always. Earlier, she had flipped the channels to try to attune me to her protective presence. And now, she was letting me know that she was still watching over me. I knew without a doubt that I could make it to the gastroenterologist's office.

I ended up spending five days in the hospital, but I had a feather that I got on Daddy's birthday!

13.

I remember the anniversary of my near-death experience every year. I have always honored the gift bestowed on me that extraordinary day. The thought of the glorious place I saw and the amazing love I felt still gives me shivers and makes my eyes misty. Nothing I ever feel in this world will even come close to matching the love, emotion, knowledge, and comfort I felt during that experience.

In this journal entry, I write about how Mother reminded me from across the veil that she knew what day it was and that she celebrated it with me. Once again, she used Bullet as a feather-detection device!

April 11, 2008

My near death-experience happened fifteen years ago on this date. Every year, the memories bring to mind all the years I spent not under- standing any of it. Because of the awareness I've gained in the last few years, I now embrace every day of living with new expectations and a new awareness. I have come so far in the past few years in this awakened life. I feel excitement with each new day at what I will learn, what I will ex- perience, or what I will be given to appreciate. My interests have totally changed and so has my way of viewing the world.

Thank heavens for the feathers, though! I don't get them everyday anymore, but I still get them sometimes in astounding ways, and today was one of them.

I have been sick for a month with pancreatitis, and this week I have had a sinus infection on top of that. This afternoon, Bullet and I went out- side for his midday constitution. It was an absolutely beautiful spring day with a few puffs of white clouds amid an otherwise pure blue sky. Bul- let had a sense that I was not feeling well so he decided to poop close to the house. He found his spot, and as I waited for him, suddenly about three feet in front of me and about the same distance over my head, I saw a feather being blown through the air. It floated on the wind, tossing to and fro, never overturning from its upward tilt.

I stood in amazement as the wind brought it closer and closer to me. I reached above me several inches to try to catch it, but it quickly escaped. On one final attempt to catch it, I watched it drift through the fingers of my right hand and land on my shirt, sticking to the material. As I went to pull it off, I realized it was lying directly over my heart. Definitely no ac- cident! Stunned, I begin to cry and thanked Mother out loud for her guid- ing presence.

It was a bluebird feather. Mother and I loved bluebirds and had all kinds of houses for them when we lived next door to each other on the farm. When Randy and I moved to the new house, a friend built some bluebird houses for me. Seeing so many bluebirds here the first spring, I wanted to surround the yard with houses for them.

*People can say that what just happened with the feather is a coincidence, but I know better. A few years ago, I would have thought the same thing, but not anymore. That feather landed on my shirt and right over my heart because it was supposed to do so. It is direct communication through the veil—**a veil of love between two souls who miss each other, from one heart to another heart.***

14.

When I wrote this journal entry, Randy and I had just come home from our first vacation in more than two years. We had been in dire need of some fun, so we decided to go to Savannah, Georgia, where we planned to enjoy the beauty, fun, and good food of our favorite city. (Or rather, *Randy* was planning to enjoy the good food!)

The trip turned out to be filled with feathers. One day while taking a walk along one of our favorite streets, we found seven feathers. They appeared one right after the other, leading us on a trail. As always, I picked them up as we continued to walk. The last feather was about ten feet in front of our favorite place for tea! We laughed about where they had led us as we went inside to enjoy a cold, refreshing glass of peach tea. Mother was probably moving her feather spirit along in front of us with the message to keep hydrated on such a hot day!

June 22, 2008

I began to feel better by the end of May. Randy took me to Savannah on June 8ᵗʰ. I knew the trip was going to be relaxing and fun as soon as we parked the car in front of our rental house, because when I stepped outside the car, I saw a feather in the sandy soil where my foot touched the curb. Then, as I approached the pretty red door, I found another feather on the stoop. Two feathers in a matter of seconds! Mother left us feather trails all week long. (And even on the morning after we got back home, I found a feather on the patio table, waiting to welcome us and acknowledge our safe trip back!)

On this trip, we went to Tybee for the first time, and I found a feather while walking the beach. We ate at Uncle Bubba's and then drove out to the public beach. The sand was damp and the water lapped across our bare feet as we walked. I stopped for a moment and stood watching the water run back and forth across my feet, when all of a sudden a feather appeared at my left foot as the water washed back out. We were amazed that the water didn't wash it away. Randy and I were both laughing as I reached down to pick it up.

All week long, whenever I found a feather, I put it into an envelope to keep. By the time we arrived home, I had collected 19.

15.

My illness has always served as a learning tool that forces me to slow down and appreciate the little things the Universe does for me. The first few years I was sick, I felt sorry for myself because of all the things I couldn't do anymore. But by the time I wrote this journal entry, I was grateful for the *new* things I could do, and for all the things I'd learned in the meantime.

This entry wasn't as much about finding the feather as it was about the connection we have with others and the role we play in each other's lives. Here, I wrote about the remarkable surgeon who diagnosed my pancreatitis and conducted several surgeries on me for complications deriving from it, and about his nursing assistant Ann, who over time had become a friend. This story brought home to me the sweetness of life and relationships, and how as humans we are all intertwined.

October 1, 2008

I went into the hospital with pancreatitis on September 19, and I came home on the 23rd. A few days later, I still wasn't feeling well. On Monday the 29th, my friend Ann from Dr. S's office called just say hello. She hadn't even known I had been sick but could tell from the weakness in my voice that something was wrong.

I explained that my gastroenterologist had kept me in the hospital for five days, but I still wasn't feeling well. Knowing my history, Ann made me promise to come in that afternoon for an amylase and lipase blood test. The results took about two hours, and upon receiving them, Dr S wanted me to go directly to the hospital. I told him, "No, I'm going home and will come back in the morning." I knew when to admit the pain was out of control, but I needed to have a heart-to-heart discussion with Randy before being admitted to the hospital for a second time within a three-week period.

On Tuesday morning, I prepared for yet another hospital stay, hoping with all my heart it would be a short one. Yet knowing how thorough Dr. S is, I had my doubts about how short it would turn out to be. Dr. S is a bulldog when he grabs hold of a patient and only lets go when he is cer-

tain of all the facts and options. He is by far the most conscientious doctor I've ever met, and he has a loving bedside manner, as well. Most of his subordinates would not agree with his mannerisms, but they do not realize he gives only the best while expecting everyone else to share the same dedication. Being the same kind of person myself, I understand that all people don't share the same concept of dedication, but I admire him greatly for it.

When I returned to the doctor's office as promised, I was unable to convince him to let me ride this one out at home. So doctor's orders in hand, I retrieved my overnight bag from the car and walked toward the entrance to the hospital. I was about 25 feet from the main entrance when I caught sight of something moving out of the corner of my eye. As I looked down, a white feather about three inches long blew up from the ground and landed on my shoe! I saw no other feathers around and the wind was not blowing. Mother was trying to let me know she was with me, as always. I picked up the feather and put it in my purse as I thanked her for the sign of her presence.

There is always a sign! Sometimes we recognize it when it happens and other times we don't figure it out until later on after the event has passed. But we are always guided on our path if we are in awareness. I pray to stay in that awareness. I find it most reassuring.

Dr. S did let me come home after a week, and we had a serious discussion about possible surgery in the future. I will decline to have surgery as long as I can.

I have received many feathers from Mother since getting back home once again. Three are black and one is black with a white tip.

16.

This journal entry was written on my first day back home after the second hospitalization I described in the last entry. I really had been very sick, lying around with nothing to eat, and suffering lots of pain. But as the normal sounds of the house began to erase the hospital static from my head, I became overwhelmed with gratitude—for the Universe, for Randy, and also for Bullet (who was applying pressure for the appreciation he, too, so richly deserved).

This story didn't involve a feather, but it was a powerful reminder of the experience of feeling unconditional love. How welcome are the arms of home after an extended stay of any sort away from peacefulness and familiarity! Home was indeed where my heart was.

My professional life had been my priority until 1998, when I finally had to admit that working in a stress-filled environment was aggravating my illness. By the time I wrote this entry, I was beginning to appreciate that my pancreatic divisum had forced me to slow down, thereby allowing me to come to terms with my life's true purpose.

In the nearly ten years that had passed since I quit work, I had learned so much about my path and my soul. I also learned that Randy was an integral part of a lesson that involved forcing me to graciously accept love—something I had been very resistant about. And not only did I get a lesson in *accepting* love, I got a lesson in feeling I *deserved* it. I was finally at a place where both accepting love and giving it away felt the same.

October 7, 2008
I just got home from another weeklong stay in the hospital. I had so

much time to think while lying in bed—about the state of the economy, the politics of the presidential race, wars across the universe, hunger and homelessness, and finally the actual crux of life. Gosh, how I hate it when the brain has nothing to keep it occupied!

Randy was taking care of everything that needed to be done at home. He was reminded for yet another week of what it takes to run the household. He is so good to Bullet and me. It takes time to do the ordinary tasks that keep the household functioning without turmoil. He likes it clean inside and outside; and in the past three weeks, he has remembered how hard and how much time is required to keep it that way. The laundry, the dog, the yard, the cleaning all have to be done almost every day or otherwise there's hell to pay the next day!

As always, he did an incredible job with the chores, considering he also worked his usual 50- to 60-hour week and visited me in the hospital. It took great multi-tasking on his part, but then again, he does that every day for 12 to 18 hours at work! He has been an excellent provider and husband for 16 years.

I am in the midst of seeking answers to several questions about my spiritual path and where it leads. I know the path is right but don't understand the constant delays the pancreatitis brings. In the future, I want to better control my health needs. I want to listen to my body and know that it is okay for me to have down time and not constantly seek to be the Energizer Bunny.

I know finishing my book is part of my future. I want to be able to look to that future without thinking of the pancreatitis as a deterrent, because after all, it is the stimulus to the whole awakening. Ironic, isn't it? Something that can make you feel so bad that you want to die ends up making you happier than you've ever been and filling you with gratitude.

As I sit here listening to the noise from Randy vacuuming and Bul-

let chomping on his bone beside my feet, I think how lucky I am to have these two beings who love me so much. Both he and Bullet are so happy to have me home. And in turn, they continue to be the reason I get up every morning. I don't mean to sound so melodramatic, but I can't help thinking about what would have happened to me over the past 16 years if I had not had Randy to love and care for me. I have also had the love of several great dogs. And I can't possibly imagine living without the Divine love that continues to come to me in more ways than one!

17.

Thanksgiving and Christmas were on the way entirely too soon. I still wasn't feeling well, and I was worried about how I was going to get ready for Thanksgiving the following Thursday. I was also worrying about needing to shop and decorate for Christmas, cook during the holidays, and still be able to feel like enjoying the fun!

Somewhere in all of these wild worries and anxious thoughts, the Universe knew I needed to be reminded that everything always works out as it should. All my fretting was merely filling my receptors with worry, confusion, and self-induced stress. So, naturally, Mother provided a rest from the worry with one of her famous feather flights!

Friday was my day out of the house. My favorite thing to do on these days was to go to Barnes & Noble, sit at a small table, and write in my journal. On this day, I was working on an exercise in forgiveness that my intuitive counselor had assigned me. As I sat there gazing out the window, deciding how to phrase my words correctly, the worry thoughts began their journey through my mind — at least until Mother decided to get my attention!

November 21, 2008

*Today I am sitting at Barnes & Noble. It is noon and the day is ex-
tremely cold. The wind is blowing out of the northeast, blustery and frigid,
chilling me to the bone. The sun is trying unsuccessfully to peek through
the heavy and dark gray-blue clouds.*

*As I sat here writing about the people I need to forgive and the
things that I need to let go of, I was staring out of the large window at the
traffic on the four-lane street out front, almost as if I was in some kind of
trance. Suddenly the wind began to blow viciously, and I heard it whis-
tling as it penetrated the miniscule cracks in the windowpane's insulation.*

*While I sat staring out toward the sidewalk, I was brought back into
the moment when the wind blew a small solid white feather right in front
of me. The wind held the feather at the perfect spot right in front of my
eyes so there was no way to miss it. I smiled and telepathically thanked
Mother for her presence. Immediately, the following words rang through
my brain: "Connie, stop worrying!" It was as if I actually heard her voice
speaking to me. Seeing that she is the one who taught me about worrying,
I guess she should be the one to tell me to stop!*

*I watched the feather, and just as suddenly as it appeared, it was
gone and the wind was quieted again!* Absolutely wonderful! *Mother used the feather to get my attention so she could capture my clear mind
long enough to send the thought-message to my brain!* **Worry never
helps.**

Thanksgiving went off without a hitch! I decorated the house
for Christmas on Friday and into the weekend. The trees were up
and the lights were on our huge front door, and all looked magnifi-

cent! The bows were on the mailbox and the lamppost. Yes, Christmas was going to get here, just like Thanksgiving, and all was going to be fine!

part three

From Grief
to a New Reality

Introduction to Part Three

When this project began, the first few paragraphs and pages appeared on paper like the wind blowing across the desert, meeting no obstacles and gathering strength as it came. The wind changed directions from time to time, causing me to lose momentum and to question if this was what I was really destined to do. Yet within the storms that arose, I found love, forgiveness, peace, contentment, and purpose.

As the months turned into years, the pattern of it all came to light. I found that the obstacles were really more like learning experiences forcing me to see an even greater need for the words on the pages. Heartbreak? Yes, it teaches us to cope. Sickness? Yes, it teaches us that we can be strong. Grief? Yes, it teaches us different lessons within each stage, and ultimately we find our *healing* through the hurt. What I learned during this experience is that through *anything*, we can learn to move ahead. And in the process of moving forward, we realize that what we go through is often a piece of cake compared to what someone else may be experiencing! Suddenly, we find empathy in the midst of our struggles, and a new awareness comes forth.

In Part Three, I share a few more stories that illustrate the process of integrating my heartbreak, sickness, and grief with the love, encouragement, and awareness that grew out of it. This is about moving forward into what's next, slowly at first and with more assurance as time goes on. It's not without irony that I admit that I, who have always been leery of new beginnings, now actually find myself embracing them.

Chapter Five:
Scrambled Eggs and Grief

The year Mother died, I missed her deeply, but I also accepted very matter-of-factly that she was gone and could not begin to contemplate mourning her loss. I didn't even really have a good cry about it. After experiencing near death more than once, I *knew* the relief that came from no longer being in physical pain. Mother had fought her entire life with body and soul to overcome both emotional and physical challenges that required constant healing. For the most part, she did a marvelous job, but it must have been exhausting. Now that she was free of that misery, how could I possibly wish that she were back here again? Was it even fair of me to regret that she was gone from this world? The idea of mourning her seemed so selfish.

All that changed on my first Thanksgiving without her, six months after she died. The immediate family and some of our dearest friends were coming to our house for a holiday lunch—20 people in all. I had never cooked a turkey, so my sister was going to do the honors. We usually had Mother's famous chicken and dumplings, but since neither my sister nor I had learned how she made them, Thanksgiving would have to go on without them. (We had naively thought Mother would live forever, and so there would always be another time to learn.) I did my part by baking the desserts and making a pleasant place for the meal.

Because we lived in a very small house, we needed to rearrange things so that we'd have enough space for everyone to sit. Randy and I had worked into the wee hours of the morning the night before the holiday, switching the furniture in the dining and living rooms. We moved our large rectangular dining table and two smaller round tables into the living room, with its stone fireplace as the focal point. It seemed like the coziest of restaurants! We planned to build a fire, not only to warm the room, but also to create more ambiance. Our best china, stemware, table linens, decorations, and candles would also contribute to the atmosphere. Quite pleased with our success, we went to bed for a few winks of sleep before I began cooking.

On Thanksgiving morning, I started making a scrambled-egg breakfast for Randy. I melted a small amount of butter in the skillet as I cracked two eggs into a bowl and began to whip them, just like always. I poured the whipped mixture into the warm skillet, and at the same moment that I heard the sizzling sound of the eggs beginning to cook, I suddenly became overwhelmed with grief. In that split second, the flood of tears I had been holding back for six months came rushing to the surface, and I fell to my knees, crying out in a mournful scream.

Alarmed, Randy ran into the kitchen to find me sitting in the middle of the floor, sobbing uncontrollably. As tears dripped down my chin, Bullet stood next to me licking them away. Randy held me all the while, not having any idea what was wrong. He just knew that when the flow of tears stopped, he would get an explanation.

Mother had taught me how to scramble eggs when I was young so that I could feed our dog Tiny, who was a picky eater, before I left for school on the mornings when she was at work. (She worked alternating shifts at the hospital and so wasn't always home when it was time to feed the dog.). Mother had showed me the process of whipping the eggs to just the right consistency, keeping them fluffy without adding milk. She taught me just the right number of shakes required from the saltshaker.

For almost 50 years, I'd been scrambling eggs exactly the way she taught me. On that particular morning, the sound of the eggs cooking had without any warning loosened an avalanche of memories—and simultaneously, the reality of my loss hit me. Mother wasn't going to be there. There wasn't going to be any chicken and dumplings or homemade yeast rolls! Her apron would stay folded in the kitchen drawer at Daddy's house. There would be no beautifully flushed face in the kitchen creating all the scrumptious smells we had come to associate with Thanksgiving.

At that moment, I was able to mourn without any guilt. I realized then that it was not selfish to grieve for my loss, but rather totally *un*selfish to remember and appreciate all that Mother had taught me while she was here. In that way, grief is actually a tribute to our loved ones! After all, we couldn't feel grief unless we had first felt a lot of love.

That's how I burned my first batch of eggs on Thanksgiving morning! Now, I smile when I scramble eggs, not really because of the eggs, but because I remember the love that Mother put into them—even for the dog! It spoke volumes about her character.

It would be two more years before Mother would gift me with the feather on the boot and show me that she was always with me, even though she was now on the Other Side. But even so, in the pain of that holiday morning, I found my heart filled with her presence because it was filled with her love.

Chapter Six:
Shower of Blessings

On December 4, 2008, I fell in the shower. It was about 4:20 p.m. I was taking my shower before *Hardball* came on so I could find out the latest political news from Chris Matthews. But the Universe had an entirely different plan in mind for me.

Before it happened, I'd been in the middle of shampooing my hair. I decided I was too cold because the exhaust fan was sucking all the warmth out of the shower stall, so I opened the shower door and reached for the switch just outside to turn the fan off. But as did so, I slipped (probably because of the shampoo suds on the shower floor) and fell. I tried to find something to grab to break the fall, but there wasn't a thing to hold on to. I remember thinking in mid-fall, *Oh God, this is going to hurt!* That was my last thought until I woke up an hour later.

Eventually, I became aware that my right ear was experiencing the grossest "wet willie" that anyone could possibly imagine. Through the foggy vision I had in that moment, I saw Bullet hovering over me. He was suddenly nose-to-nose with me and wagging his tail and wiggling all over. (Randy and I call it a waggle!)

I suppose all dogs have personality quirks. Bullet would go after one of his stuffed animal toys when he thought someone was upset with him or wasn't paying him enough attention. When I came to enough to take a look around me, I found that I was surrounded by every stuffed toy he owned. Trust me, emptying his toy box must have taken a while! I am sure he heard all the noise I made as I was falling, and he must have heard me moaning in pain while I was unconscious. So he tried to wake me up the only way he knew how.

Lying naked with half my body in the shower and the other half on the tile floor, I realized how very cold I was. The door was open to the shower, and the running water was now freezing cold. And my body hurt all over! Immediately realizing my ribs were broken and that I had a punctured lung, I was also on the verge of shock. I crawled to the phone and called Randy. Luckily, he was only a ten-minute drive away. I managed to dress myself while he was driving home. I still don't know how I got up and put my clothes on, but I did.

I spent a week in the hospital. I was not allowed to get out of bed for anything, and my bruised and broken body ached! Randy and I never realized how battered my body was until after I got home from the hospital because my ribs hurt so bad that I couldn't pay attention to anything else at first. The effects began to appear one day at a time: we discovered that my scalp had been bleeding, my left hip and buttock were blue all the way down to my knee, and my teeth began to fall out or get loose. Only Randy and I knew how really lucky I had been.

Bullet truly had saved my life that afternoon. He was my hero, and for the rest of his life, if I so much as dropped the soap in the shower, he would come running to check it out.

The fall meant another long delay for the book, but by this time I had much more understanding of why life was the way it was! The Universe was speaking loudly, and I listened. I gave myself permission to rest and heal. The healing time turned into months (I still have aches and pains as a result of that fall), but as the quietness required to help me heal became my teacher, I realized there was a purpose! The idea for the rest of my book came to me during that time, and I was shown what I was supposed to do. I would dream as I napped, and the dreams would provide answers. I'm not glad I had to go through the pain of the fall, but I am delighted I went through the healing time slowly and purposefully.

That year, Randy and I had a quiet Christmas Day and thoroughly enjoyed it. We got just what we needed for Christmas—time together and an incredible feeling of appreciation for how lucky I had been (not just this time, but many other times when the Universe has taken care of me, as well). We made sure, however, that we got one Christmas gift to put under the tree—a new toy and a bone for Bullet!

My custom had always been to take the tree down the day after Christmas, although Randy routinely begged me to leave it up a little longer. That Christmas, he got his wish. We kept the Christmas tree up until the end of February! And I didn't worry about it a bit. I was happy just to be alive.

Chapter Seven:
Two Feathered Mother's Days

Even before Mother died, Mother's Day had long held a palpable sadness for me—ever since I'd had a full-term stillborn when I was 23. I'd found out only two days before the baby was born that the child was already dead. I'd been devastated.

Mother was the only one in the family who honored me every Mother's Day. She alone had been the one to understand my ability to feel like a mother even though I had known the child in my womb for only nine months. She recognized that to me, this had been my little boy, and he had had a personality. He had been active at the same exact time every day, and quiet at certain other times—always predictable and on schedule. During the pregnancy, I felt as if I knew him in a very real way, even though I'd not laid eyes on him yet.

Mother knew what it meant for another being to live inside you, draw from your energy supply, and communicate with you before he or she was even born. So every Mother's Day, she had sent me flowers or a card with beautiful words about what a good mother I would have been if motherhood had been "written in the heavens" for me. But after 2003, the cards and flowers stopped. And every Mother's Day since, remembering those heartfelt gestures of love and support, I have missed her even more than usual.

Randy's mother had been very close to her own mother, so Mother's Day became difficult for her, as well, after Randy's grandmother died. So we started a tradition of his family coming to our house for lunch on Mother's Day. Focusing on the cooking provided a good distraction for me, so the new custom proved to be good for both of us.

The Friday afternoon before Mother's Day 2009, as I began to dust and vacuum in preparation for having company, I caught myself laughing. I realized that the old adage about when daughters get older, they became their mothers had indeed happened to me! Whenever Mother had expected company, everything in the house had to be spotless. God bless us all if company saw any dust bunnies in her house! Unfortunately, I inherited this fixation. As the thought processes in my head moved along, I jokingly thanked her out loud for giving me her hips, too!

After I had dusted everything else, I turned my attention to the bookcase. I began working my way down the sides and finally onto the shelving and books. As I got to the third shelf, I gasped. There was a white feather about three inches long lying in front of the clock—a feather that I'd not put there or seen before. Suddenly, I began to laugh aloud from down deep within my belly. It occurred to me that Mother had heard me fussing about having inherited my anal retentive cleaning bug from her! Unfortunately, she probably heard the comment about the hips, too!

The feather still lies there, right where I found it. Every time I dust, I pick it up and smile at the memory of the day she left it for me to chide me about how fastidious I can become about things that aren't really all that important. What *is* important is enjoying being with family while we can—not eliminating the dust bunnies. (After all, they don't really take up that much space anyway!)

The following year, I was cleaning again on the Friday before Mother's Day. (Some habits die hard!) Smiling as always when I dusted the shelves, I picked up the white feather to enjoy the loving memory of its arrival. But much to my surprise, when I picked it up I found *another* smaller feather hidden underneath it—a perfect, inch-long blue jay feather. I was absolutely certain that the smaller feather had not been there when I had dusted two weeks earlier. *Feather number one* of that Mother's Day weekend. Delighted at the new arrival, I decided to leave the two feathers together on that shelf in front of the clock. (And they're still there to this day; even though we've moved since then, I carefully transported them and made sure I placed them back in the spot where I originally found them.)

Randy had taken the day off on Saturday to help me prepare for the family visit. Since I had cleaned the upstairs on Friday, Randy helped me clean the main living area on Saturday. It was no easy task, partly because when Randy was off from work, Bullet always demanded his full attention. This day was no exception. Bullet got into everything. He had removed his doggie toys from their basket and stood at the door wanting to go outside every 30 minutes. He acted like a three-year-old who couldn't make up his mind whether he wanted to play outside or inside.

When we finished cleaning, I noticed something odd on the hardwood floor. At first, I thought it was just an unusual grain in the wood that I had never noticed before. When I bent over for a closer look, I realized it was a miniscule feather, about one inch long. It couldn't have been there long because Randy had just cleaned the floor! As I picked it up and held it above my head, Randy and I grinned at each other. *Feather number two!*

A few minutes later, Bullet just absolutely had to go outside. It was a gorgeous spring day with cool breezes and clear skies, but it had rained the previous night and the grass was still wet. Randy took the dog outside while I waited just inside the door with a towel to dry off his feet when he came in so he wouldn't dirty Randy's clean floor. We had a routine about wiping off his feet, so when he came back inside, Bullet obliged me. He stood still while I picked up each of his paws to dry them off.

When I picked up the last paw, a five-inch-long brown feather fell to the floor from his furry foot! *Feather number three!* Randy just stood there and looked at the smug grin I had on my face.

"Mother wants me to know she was here and that she knows Mother's Day is tomorrow," I told him, and he agreed. I proceeded to put the larger feather with the very tiny one I had found earlier, promptly taking them upstairs to my desk for safekeeping.

The next morning, before everyone arrived, we admired how pretty all the tables looked with their decorations. We had a table set up in the dining room, one on the sun porch, and one outside on the patio. All three were arranged differently with fresh flowers from my garden. Each table contained different china, glassware, and linens. The colors blended and the presentation was excellent. I had enjoyed every minute of prepping them.

As usual, we had a great time with Randy's family, but we were ready for the quiet when everyone left. Randy and I had entertained so often that we had a schedule for who does what with clean up, and each of us began our customary duties: I collected and he cleaned. I began with the table on the sun porch, clearing the table completely of all the dishes. After putting away all of the charger plates, I moved the vase of flowers to a different table so I could remove the dirty tablecloth and take it to the laundry room.

When I turned around from moving the flowers, there lying

in the middle of the table was a little whitish-gray feather. *Feather number four!* Before removing it from the tablecloth, I shouted for Randy to come to the sun porch and see it! He looked at it with the same amazement I did.

"Your Mother was really trying to let you know she was with us this weekend," he told me, and I had to heartily agree. I put the feather on the granite ledge between the kitchen and the living room as I made my way down the hall to the laundry room with the tablecloth.

Then I returned to the sun porch to move the table back into its usual position. While reaching down to move the rug from underneath the table, I found another feather! It was about four inches long and the same whitish-gray color as the one I had just found on the tablecloth only moments before. The two feathers looked so alike that I got confused, thinking maybe it was the same feather and that it had attached to my clothes with static electricity and fallen off when I bent over to move the rug.

Holding it tightly in my hand, I went into the kitchen. But sure enough, the feather I found earlier was lying right where I had put it moments before. I began to laugh aloud and showed it to Randy, explaining how I had found it on the rug underneath the table. *Feather number five!* We both said hello to Mother and continued to clean up.

I next went outside to begin the task of breaking down the table on the patio, which we had ended up not using. I stood there admiring how beautiful it was and what a great job I had done on designing the flowers for it. The tablecloth was navy with a white intersecting stripe. The chargers were silver, and the plates were white. The gold napkins, which I'd placed on top of the plates, were held in the middle by blue and white porcelain napkin rings. Three blue and white vases of differing shapes sat in the center of the table, all filled with white mock orange and stems of honeysuckle. The tiny tinges of gold inside the mock orange blossom and the gold of the honeysuckle made the napkins look perfect. The whole presentation was awesome. Because no one had eaten here, I had been able to enjoy the beauty of my creation all day!

I began putting everything away and re-arranging the table's usual décor. After having made several trips in and out the door and back and forth to the kitchen, I was on my last trip. I closed the door behind me, locking it for the evening. I took my shoes off and went to put them where I always keep them, atop the brick floor of the sun porch, when I saw yet another feather on the brick. *Feather number six!*

When I had put my shoes on so I could go outside, the feather had *not* been there. And I had been in and out of that door at least six times without seeing anything! Clearly, Mother had placed the feather there, knowing I wouldn't miss it when I removed my shoes and put them in their place. *Just how much does she watch us anyway?* I thought to myself. *Clearly she remembers that I am a creature of habit!*

Pointing to the feather, I showed the prize to Randy and stared at it in disbelief for a few seconds before I finally picked it up. Randy gave me a loving hug, letting me savor all the beautiful moments that had transpired that day. I couldn't hold back the tears of joy any longer.

It had been an awesome weekend of communication with Mother—starting with the blue jay feather in the bookcase. She was letting me know that she had seen the three gorgeous tables and was proud of my creative talent, but also that she still thinks of me on Mother's Day and remembers what that means to me.

Epilogue:
My Journey and What *I Know that I Know*

Writing this book has been quite the journey for my soul, a journey that continues to astound me. As I lived these stories and learned their lessons, I came to understand myself and to change a belief system that had been in place for years. The Universe managed to teach me even through my resistance, although it certainly didn't happen overnight. Even now, for example, I wonder why it took so long after my near-death experience for me to figure out that I had indeed been worthy of living. I think the Universe was giving me the time I needed to seek out the wisdom from within my own soul. Deep down, somewhere, somehow, my soul kept on trying to tell me what I needed to know. Maybe, just maybe, I already knew some of these things and needed only to admit it.

Before I opened up to the Universe, I had a "to do" list for every day, week, month, and even year because I thought that was part of being a responsible adult. But who among us knows where he or she will be a year from now—or even tomorrow? I had some glimmers of higher truth even before I had my near-death experience in 1993, but I didn't know what to do with that knowledge. I found it difficult to operate outside of the logic of my left brain, so I engaged in a struggle that lasted for several years. The Universe would drag me back to the intuitive experiences of my right brain and try to start all over again.

I finally gave in when I found the feather on the boot, which simply allowed *no* logical explanation! I was being asked to step outside the comfort zone that I had hibernated in for a very long time. From that moment on, coincidence has no longer existed in my world. The feather on the boot was meant as a sign to let me know that it was time to move forward in my spiritual journey, and that indeed, I still had work to do. My reluctance to step out beyond the realm of what this world considers logical thinking had finally dissolved. Even if I didn't know all the answers to all my questions, of two things I became absolutely certain: Life after death exists, as does communication from the Other Side.

Now I understand fully that the Universe constantly surrounds us with signs to give us both information and comfort. We need only be open and willing to recognize who or what the Universe may be using as a communication device at any one time. Because this communication is often subtle, it is vital that we stay aware of our surroundings. The signs are always there if we choose to pay attention to them. Once we figure this out, we become more empathetic and more conscious of the respect we owe to both nature and our fellow man.

Some days I hear unusual things, some days I see unusual things, and some days I don't hear or see anything unusual at all. But when it does happen, I don't run from it or ignore it anymore. I know that in time, an explanation and an understanding will come to me. It all goes back to the metaphor of the puzzle—the pieces will never fit if I try to squeeze them into a space where they don't belong. Any piece only fits where it fits!

I also no longer worry about other people judging me. I am totally comfortable believing what I believe because after all that's happened in my 60 years, there are certain truths that *I know that I know that I know.*

No matter how hard someone may try to dissuade me, these truths will never again change for me.

I KNOW:

Forgiveness, awareness, love, and grace are astute teachers.

Everyone has the right to his own religious beliefs, even if they differ from mine (or yours). The sum of the many makes a whole.

Awareness is the gift the Universe gives us to help us find our path.

There is no such thing as coincidence.

Heaven exists, and life after death is real.

Everyone's life is full of lessons, and we are all responsible for teaching others what we have learned.

Respecting the candor and wisdom in the advice that comes from our elders as well as observing and respecting the honesty of children is vital.

Subtle but sincere communication with those who have crossed over is possible.

I may not always understand all the various nuances of these

truths, but I *know* that if I have patience and trust in the Universe, everything that I need to know will come to me.
I have seen this happen over and over again.

I remember working on this book one day in 2008, sitting with all my journals on our sun porch. The light was streaming through the windows, the birds were chirping outside, and the garden was in full bloom. There I sat in front of a huge stack of colorful, hardbound journals, waiting for something to happen. Although I'd written some parts of the book, I now needed to decide which stories from my journals were supposed to be shared, and I had no idea how I was supposed to figure that out. I had so many!

Then, just as the name of the book and the cover had come to me years before, certain stories began to appear in my mind's eye. As I picked up each journal, the stories within it that I was supposed to share just came to me. It was miraculous! The decision, after all, was up to Spirit, not me!

Likewise, the book's progress didn't always go according to my plan and the work was often delayed by my ill health. Sometimes, I'd lose my concentration for days and even months. As I've shared before, the entire focus of the project shifted throughout the process, as well. Nothing about this book is the same as my original idea. *Is it possible I had to live into and become a part of the book first? Is it possible that the reason for the health problems I began to suffer in my 40s was part of some grand plan for my soul's growth?* I have to answer those questions with a resounding YES!

I began to realize about living *into* the book and living in the moment. I learned to really appreciate life—every day of it—and that on some days, it is acceptable to *just be*. I could wait for the ability to write again. *Have patience, Connie! It will come,* I would tell myself. And it always did. The process taught me to take life in stride and be more patient not only with others (which has always been easy for me) but also with myself (which has been much more challenging).

Eventually, the Universe would begin to show the path again, and the work would continue, the words flying across the page as they did in the beginning. The delay would be yet another reminder that the Universe has its own timetable, and we are not always consulted. I came to understand that we don't always get what we want in this life, but we *do* get what we need to learn and grow spiritually. And all the while, through the times when the writing was going well and the times when I thought I'd never finish, Mother kept leaving me feathers to encourage me, to give me guidance, and to show me how much she loved me.

While mothers and daughters may not always get along with each other, I've learned that a daughter does eventually grow into her mother's shoes. In most cases, those are big shoes to fill. The older we become, the more we realize the shoes were well worn! Sometimes the soles of a mother's shoes are worn down from pacing, when she is filled with worry and anxiety. We can understand and appreciate our mothers only after we are old enough to see what they lived through and what they sacrificed for us.

A mother's love is like no other. It is as sweet as honey, yet it can sometimes sting like a bee. It is an understanding love, yet it is a most demanding one at the same time. It is ever critical, because it wants to push us to our highest potential, yet it's always hopeful because our mothers do *see* that potential, even when we can't. In a very real way, a mother's love gives birth to us. It creates us as a person. Whether the love we receive is gentle or cruel, it defines who we are. But make no mistake—whether that love came from an attentive mother or an inattentive mother, it is still one of a kind.

My mother's love molded me in many ways—some of them I like and some of them I don't. However, I loved Mother's ability to rise above her difficulties and move forward. She always did it with class and style! And she inspires me to do the same. For that, and for so many other things, I will be forever grateful to her.

By the time I finally overcame the various hurdles to completing the book and began to share more of my stories with others, I also learned that teachable moments are extremely important not only for us personally, but for everyone around us. We do not have to be professional teachers to teach what we know. The changes we make as we grow are visible to others and will attract to us exactly the right person who is in need of what we have to teach at exactly the right time—for us and for them. In fact, most of our teaching is done without us even knowing that we are teaching anyone anything! All that is required is our sincerity, which will act as a beacon. Sometimes, it's as easy as sharing a book!

Appendix:
Feather Trivia

When this feather-covered path began, I needed to learn and understand more about feathers. The more I read and searched for information, the more the Universe would easily present it, exactly the way I needed to see it. The following are a few fun facts I've found about feathers along the way.

At any one time, 400 billion birds inhabit our planet, each one covered with anywhere from one thousand to 25 thousand feathers. Just as humans keep growing hair, birds drop and replenish their feathers, a process called molting. Most birds molt once a year, although some species molt a second time. Usually, a bird will lose a few feathers at a time, most often in a symmetrical way in order to maintain the aerodynamics required for flying. If for some reason only one feather falls out, birds will often pull out the matching feather from the other side. The feathers grow back rapidly, which requires a lot of energy. Knowing how much energy is needed to replace a feather makes finding one an even more extraordinary treasure!

Feathers not only help birds fly, but they also protect them from chilly or wet weather, and their bright colors help them attract mates. Humans have also found many uses for feathers, the most profound being their use in religious and spiritual ceremonies. Many indigenous populations throughout the world associate feathers not only with flight but also with the heavens themselves, as if they could bring us closer to them. Native Americans, for example, see feathers as sacred and use them in healing ceremonies. In fact, because eagles are federally protected in the U.S., it is illegal to possess their feathers unless you are a certified and enrolled member of a federally recognized Native American tribe.

Today, we fashion jewelry and hair ornaments out of feathers, decorate clothing with them, accent flower arrangements with them, and even re-create their likeness in designs (including, for example, the drawing on the cover of this book). We have also put feathers to utilitarian use for cleaning (feather dusters), fishing (lures), and writing (quill pens). In fact, the word "pen" is derived from the Latin word *penna*, which means "feather."

Of course, feathers have also long been a favorite when making bedding. My grandmother kept chickens on her farm for their meat and eggs, and she also used their feathers to stuff pillows and mattresses. There is absolutely nothing like lying down on a feather mattress in the chill of winter and having it envelope and cradle you in warmth. When we pulled Mamaw's homemade quilts over us, as well, the combination literally surrounded us in her love! My sister still has the feather pillow Mamaw made for her (although she's put new pillow ticking over it more times than I can count). She claims she can't sleep without it.

Finally, feathers are also the subject of several colorful figures of speech, including getting one's feathers in an uproar and ruffling one's feathers—not to mention the exclamation, "Oh horsefeathers!" or the famous adage, "Birds of a feather flock together." And of course, John Wayne uttered this famous line in his role as Rooster Cogburn in the movie *True Grit*: "My tail feathers may droop a bit, and my wattles show, but I can still out-crow anything in the barnyard."

About the Author

    C.C. (Connie) Ford was born and raised in Knoxville, Tennessee. She attended the University of Tennessee for two years before beginning a three-year apprentice program at a local optical dispensary, earning her optician's license in 1975. She worked as an optician for 28 years before retiring for health reasons. She and her husband Randy still live in Knoxville, where C.C. spends as much time as she can outdoors, very often working in her garden. She estimates that her collection has now grown to at least two thousand feathers.

In, Out.
Deep, Slow.
Calm, Ease.
Smile, Release.
Present Moment, Wonderful
Moment.

CPSIA information can be obtained at www.ICGtesting.com
Printed in the USA
BVOW11s1605220714

360082BV00012B/157/P

9 781304 596840